A STUDY IN
BLACK AND WHITE

The Aborigines
in Australian History

TO THE HONOURABLE SPEAKER AND MEMBERS OF THE HOUSE OF REPRESENTATIVES
IN PARLIAMENT ASSEMBLED.

The Humble Petition of the Undersigned Aboriginal people of Yirrkala,
being members of the Balamumu, Narrkala, Gapiny, Miliwurrwurr people
and Djapu, Mangalili, Madarrpa, Magarrwanalmirri, Djambarrpuynu, Gumaitj,
Marrakulu, Galpu, Dhaluwuyu, Wangurri, Warramirri, Maymil, Ririjinga
tribes respectfully showeth.

1. That the people of the above tribes are residents of the land
    excised from the Aboriginal Reserve in Arnhem Land.
2. That the procedures of the excision of this land and the fate of the
    people on it were never explained to them beforehand, and were kept
    secret from them.
3. That when Welfare Officers and Government officials came to inform
    them of decisions taken without them and against them, they did not
    undertake to convey to the Government in Canberra the views and
    feelings of the Yirrkala Aboriginal people.
4. That the land in question has been hunting and food gathering land for
    the Yirrkala tribes from time immemorial; we were all born here.
5. That places sacred to the Yirrkala people, as well as vital to their
    livelihood are in the excised land, especially Melville Bay.
6. That the people of this area fear that their needs and interests will
    be completely ignored as they have been ignored in the past, and they
    fear that the fate which has overtaken the Larrakeah tribe will
    overtake them.
7. And they humbly pray that the Honourable the House of Representatives
    will appoint a Committee, accompanied by competent interpreters, to
    hear the views of the people of Yirrkala before permitting the
    excision of this land.
8. They humbly pray that no arrangements be entered into with any company
    which will destroy the livelihood and independence of the Yirrkala
    people.

And your petitioners as in duty bound will ever pray God to help you and us.
(English language translation.)

✳ ✳ ✳ ✳ ✳ ✳ ✳ ✳ ✳ ✳ ✳ ✳ ✳ ✳

Bukmakmiri gong'yurru napurrunha Yirrkalalili yolnuuba malnuba
Balamumu, Narrkala, Gapiny, Miliwurrwurr, napapurru Dhuwala nala, ga
Djapu, Mangalili,Madarrpa, Magarrwanalmirri, Djambarrpuynu, Marrakulu,
Gumaitj, Galpu, Dhaluwuyu, Wangurri, Warramirri, Maymil, Ririjinga
malnuranapamiri djal djapuru.

1. Dhuwala yolnu nala wekut 500 nhina ga dhuyala wangarrar, Dhuwala wanga
    Arnhem Land yurru dju'yuruu maturrugala.
2. Dhuwala wanga dju'rrunu ga dhaliinuu yurru yolnuuwudja dhiyala wanga
    nuru dhaliinuu dhu dharrpanna yolnu walangja rakuna lakaruna
    madarungununa.
3. Dhuwala nguni Welfare Officers ga Government bungawa lakaruna yolnuwu
    malannuu dhaliinuru nhuma guna napramalanu yutu nala napurrunga
    lakaruna, walala yaka lakaruna Governmentagala bunbala Canberra
    nhaliinuru napurru ga napawa yulnuya Yirrkala.
4. Dhuwala wanga napurruyu balaun larumarrawu Madarrpaya nhituwu, dhuwal
    niyungwan, napurru nuun napurru guna Nhinana Nitjarrayi nhthulilarri,
    napurru Gumaitjnurunu dhiyala, nugunwuna.
5. Dhuwala wanga yurru dharrpalnha dhuwai ninuwalanja maluwai, ga
    dharryalnha dhuwala wala yolnuwudja rakinudhuwawu Melville Baythuru
    wanga malandayu dju'rru nyuwaknuna.
6. Dhuwala yolnuudja nala yurru nuhnana balandawuna dhu ngilarru nhana
    nala nuun ga napuruu yalnilawurrinha nhaliinuna dju napurru Nitjarra
    nhana Larrakayu namuru nalalawu'nha wanga.
7. Yuli dhu bungawari House of Representatives dju'rru yolnuwala mildili
    yurru nha dhu lakaruna interpreterru bungawawudja yolnu natha, yurru dhu
    dhu dje'rrun winawudja.
8. Bundarinu dhu'wudu mardiyalu marrama'ndja nhinanharruwa yolnuwu
    marrawudhinjurraruwu.

Dhuwala napurru nala, nala napuru lirunirriyama bulnu bili narr yurru
napurru nha gong'yununa waterri'wu.
(Australian Natha.)

A STUDY IN
BLACK AND WHITE

The Aborigines
in Australian History

Third Edition

MALCOLM D. PRENTIS

ROSENBERG

(*Opposite*) The famous 'Bark Petition' of 1963, a protest at the Yolngu people's loss of land to a mining company.

In memory of Noel Prentis (1923–2007) and Claire Florence Cornelius Prentis (1923–2002), who taught me to look not on the outward appearance.

This third revised edition published in 2009 by Rosenberg Publishing Pty Ltd
PO Box 6125, Dural Delivery Centre NSW 2158
Phone: +61 2 9654 1502 Fax: +61 2 9654 1338
Email: rosenbergpub@smartchat.net.au
Web: www.rosenbergpub.com.au

First published in 1975 by Methuen Australia Pty Ltd
Second edition published in 1988 by Social Science Press

National Library of Australia Cataloguing-in-Publication data

Author: Prentis, Malcolm D. (Malcolm David), 1948-

Title: A study in black and white : Aborigines in Australia history
Malcolm D. Prentis.

Edition: 3rd ed.

ISBN: 9781877058783 (pbk.)

Notes: Includes index.
Bibliography.

Subjects: Aboriginal Australians--History.
Aboriginal Australians, Treatment of.
Aboriginal Australians--Government relations.

Dewey Number: 305.89915

Printed in Thailand by Kyodo Nation Printing Services

Contents

Preface
to the Third Edition

Many changes have occurred in Aboriginal history in the last twenty years. This means not only that history has continued to happen since 1988. It also means that there have been sharp challenges to our understanding of past events, those before and since 1988. The past itself has been even more hotly contested than before 1988 as historians and others became embroiled in the so-called 'history wars'. In these circumstances, my original ambition for this book in 1975 and 1988, that it be characterized by 'balance, concision and simplicity', seems today even more naïve and perhaps utopian than it was many years ago. The 1975 edition was aimed at Year 10 of high school. The 1988 edition was used more by Year 12 and so this edition is aimed at Year 12, first-year undergraduates as well as the general reader. I have still aimed for concision and simplicity, however.

The third edition necessarily involved more changes than did the second. I have retained the unusual two-part structure, 'Aboriginal Reactions' and 'White Reactions', but have amalgamated the original second and third chapters into a new Chapter 3, 'First Contacts'. Chapter 7, however, has been extended by twenty years. The old Chapter 10, 'Since 1937', has been divided into three: Chapter 10, 'The Assimilation Era, 1937–1960s', Chapter 11, 'The Rise of Self-Determination, 1960s-1990s' and Chapter 12, 'Mabo, Wik and

Reconciliation'. The pre-existing text has been rewritten, some sections extensively, especially in Chapters 2, 5, 6, 7, 11 and 12. I have added five new readings to cover the last twenty years, three in Part One and two in Part Two. A lot more illustrations have been added and they have been used to fill out the narrative somewhat. 'Further Reading' and 'Additional References' have been revised but some of the older books remain the best. The same cannot be said about audio-visual materials, as the technology has undergone revolutionary change in twenty years and so films, websites, CD-ROMs and DVDs have been added to replace resources employing outmoded technologies. The overall result is an edition about 60 per cent longer than its predecessor.

I need to explain that some of the terminology used in this book might be deemed offensive. Usually, that is because the terms used are historical, belonging to a particular era, and it would be unhistorical and misleading to change documents and quotations. Examples of this are lower case 'aboriginal' and 'half-caste'. In general, the terminology followed here is 'Aboriginal' (adjective and singular noun), 'Aborigines' (plural noun) or 'Aboriginal people' (collective term). Unless the context indicates otherwise, 'Indigenous' is used to include all Indigenous people but this book does not deal much with the Torres Strait Islanders until the Mabo case.

Those people offended by the mention of the names or pictures of deceased Indigenous persons should not read this book.

Acknowledgments

I should like to give special thanks to my students, on-campus and otherwise, especially my Aboriginal students since 1990, including Dhangati, Ngaku, Bandjalang, Gidabal, Gamilaroi, Anaiwan, Barkindji, Wiradjuri, Biripi, Worimi, Murawari, Gumbainggar, Wonnarua and Yuin people. Working with students from Moree, Kempsey, Bourke, Boggabilla, Ivanhoe, Sydney, Bowraville, Casino, Coffs Harbour, Wilcannia and elsewhere has been very enlightening. I thank them all for what we have learned together. Conversations with Ken Ralph and other Australian Catholic University colleagues involved in Aboriginal education over the years have also been very helpful. ACU also assisted with study leave and inter-library loans.

For the earlier editions, Miss Kaye Mundine, editor of *New Dawn*, gave permission to reproduce the poem 'Aborigines'. I am grateful to Carl Harrison-Ford for his meticulous editing.

Illustrations

The author himself provided the following: Map 1 and pictures on pages 24, 30, 94 bottom and 147 bottom. Malcolm and David Prentis created maps 2, 3, 4, 5 and 6. Thanks, Dave.

The author acknowledges with thanks the providers of the illustrations as listed below for permission to reproduce.

State Library of Queensland: p. 64 bottom (60511), p. 77 (24048), p. 77 (24048) and p. 122 (10685).
State Library of Tasmania (Allport Library and Museum): cover (AUTAS00112 4071622) and p. 114 (AUTAS001125883322).
State Library of Victoria, Pictures Collection: p. 135 (H21074).
Pictures in the **public domain** are those on pages 17, 19 top, 19 bottom, 68, 88, 115 bottom, 130, 137 bottom and 147 top, plus these from Wikimedia Commons on pages 21, 34 bottom, 41 top, 41 bottom, 46, 111, 113 bottom, 115 top, 129 and 159.
In some cases, genuine attempts to trace the copyright holder have been unsuccessful. In others, the origin is simply unknown. Either or both of these apply to pictures on pages 61, 79 and 156 (a variety of slightly different versions of this exist but I have been unable to trace or get a response about this one), 169 top and 173. If the author is mistaken about the status or provenance of any of the pictures, he apologizes and undertakes to give due acknowledgment.

LIST OF READINGS

PART ONE

PART TWO

LIST OF MAPS

LISTS OF FURTHER READING

1 Introduction

The aim of this book is to make possible a clearer understanding of the present racial situation in Australia by presenting an account of its historical development from the time of Governor Phillip. Firstly, from the Aboriginal point of view, there was the situation resulting from the arrival of an alien group with an alien civilization, which dispossessed and dominated them. The first part of the book is concerned with the Aborigines' reaction to this situation and the consequences for them. Secondly, from the aliens' point of view, there was the problem of how to deal with what they saw as a 'primitive race' which they were entitled to supplant but which was capable of both attacking them and stirring their consciences. The second part of the book is concerned with the attitudes, policies and actions towards the Aborigines — of governments, other bodies and private citizens.

Invasion
In 1788 Australia became a multi-racial country without its original inhabitants being consulted. So, from the very beginning of modern Australian history, race has been a reality with which Australians have had to cope.

Something in human nature makes it hard enough for groups of people to live together happily, but it is much more difficult when two groups with radically different cultures and ways of life come into contact. To some Europeans, it was a law of nature that they, the superior group, would destroy or absorb the inferior group (the Aborigines).

Even those Europeans who were more sympathetic and wanted to protect them felt that Aborigines should become 'black Europeans' by adopting the 'superior' way of life. It is remarkable that this, or a similar view, was the basis of official policy from almost the beginning until the 1960s. When Aborigines have refused to be Europeanized, even if they wished to keep some of their traditional ways along with accepting some of the new, Western ways, they have often been regarded as misguided.

Race and Racism

'Race' and 'racism' are two widely misunderstood words. When people speak of 'race', they can be referring to any of a number of different kinds of differences between human groups (for example, cultural, colour). It is obvious that there are human groups which are physically different from each other, such as Negroes and Caucasians. In this sense, the word 'race' refers to something real.

However, such physical differences are not inherently tied to differences in culture or in social, mental or manual abilities. The belief that physical differences do determine non-physical character or various abilities is called 'racism'. Therefore, a 'racist' is someone who believes that physical characteristics are a proper basis for making legal and social distinctions between groups. In other words, he or she favours racial discrimination. In the distant past, when physical differences were often associated with significant cultural differences, it could seem reasonable to be racist. Gradually, in the last two hundred years or so, most people have come to know better, although practice has lagged behind preaching.

Then, there is also the belief in the superiority of one's culture, an attitude which is referred to as ethnocentrism. Commonly in the past, attitudes of racial superiority (racism) and cultural superiority (ethnocentrism) have gone together. It is, of course, possible to reject racism and yet believe that one's culture is superior to those of others, even if individuals of different races are seen as inherently equal. (Otherwise, what would be the point of Christian missionary activity, for instance?) However these attitudes have played out in practice, relations between Indigenous and other Australians are part of world-wide patterns of race, racism and ethnocentrism.

The British Empire

The history of the relations between Aborigines and Europeans can also be seen in the context of European imperial expansion and colonization. Though there are considerable differences in detail, the occupation of the Australian continent by Europeans is basically similar to their takeover of parts of America, Africa and Asia at about the same time. This global expansion of European power happened in a period of economic and industrial growth. It is unlikely that this was a coincidence, for expanding economic activity meant a demand for raw materials (minerals, cotton and so on), food and clothing for a growing work force, and more places to sell industrial products. Overseas expansion provided these — and also glory for adventurers.

Also during the late eighteenth and early nineteenth centuries, particularly in Britain, there was an evangelical revival and, through the so-called 'humanitarian movement', the re-awakening of Christian responsibility for various vulnerable kinds of people who were liable to be exploited. Not only did this movement result in limits on the use of child labour, shorter hours of work, the freeing of slaves, prison reform and so on; it also involved taking material and spiritual help to the 'heathens' of America, Africa, Asia and the Pacific by missionaries. Thus both economic and religious motives were often to be found behind European expansion into other parts of the world.

Naturally, the motives for taking over particular territories varied a great deal. The decision by the British government to colonize Australia was not taken for religious reasons, nor do economic motives seem to have been very important. Though there is some disagreement about it, the main reason seems to have been to get rid of an over-large gaol population. At certain stages, however, economic motives became more important, as sometimes did religious or humanitarian ones. Undoubtedly there was a vague belief in a God-given responsibility to improve or develop 'unoccupied' land, and this went hand in hand with the idea of a civilizing mission.

The mixed motives for European expansion are illustrated by the instructions given to Captain Cook in 1768 when he left on the voyage during which he discovered the land he called New South Wales. The instructions mentioned the need for careful scientific observation of the geographic features of the unknown south land, as well as the hope that the land might have valuable natural resources. Cook was also instructed to seek good relations with the natives, which he did. However, he disobeyed other orders by taking possession of the eastern side of Australia for the King without the consent of

'An Aboriginal view of Cook's statue.' In 1866, when it was proposed to erect a statue in Sydney to honour Captain Cook's 'discovery' of 1770, a white cartoonist tried to look at it from an Indigenous point of view. (*Sydney Punch*, 1866)

the natives. To the Europeans, it seemed impossible to bargain with Aborigines, who lacked obvious leaders.

This was but one misunderstanding. Relations between the Aborigines and Europeans settlers of Australia have been harmed from the beginning by one misunderstanding after another. To Europeans, civilization meant European civilization. A group could be recognized if it had a leader and if it owned, controlled and used land. Naturally, all land was held by individuals; if land was 'public' this just meant it was owned by the King. The Aborigines not only seemed to lack the appearances of 'civilization' — such as clothes, writing, agriculture and religion — but also seemed to have no king and apparently neither owned nor used land. So, obviously, most Europeans could not see the need for agreements with Aborigines before taking the land. In fact, agreements did not seem possible. Now that more is known about traditional Aboriginal society, we can see that these misunderstandings were at the root of most of the later strife. There may have been some excuse for our forerunners' making these mistakes, but there is no excuse for us today.

Land

Thus, behind the settlement of Australia by Europeans was the usually unspoken belief that the Aborigines did not 'own' the land. (In later years, the Latin term *terra nullius* or 'land of no one' was coined to describe this attitude.) This is only true, of course, if we define 'ownership' in the European sense; but it was confirmed by English law when Cook took possession of Australia, contrary to his instructions. Not only was this the belief of the government: most European settlers could not see that the Aborigines 'used' the land, either. After all, they did not sow or reap, graze sheep or plant vegetables. In fact, of course, all human groups depend on the land, in different ways and to varying degrees. This was also true of the Aborigines; however, the unusual nature of their dependence made it difficult for the Europeans to recognize it.

The Aborigines reacted as any other human group would when deprived of land: they hit back. Because the Europeans often did not realize what they had done, they felt the Aborigines had no good cause

'His Native Land. "Poor Pfella Me!" Whomever Australia is for, it is clearly not for the Australian Aboriginal.' *The Bulletin* cartoonist Phil May commented in 1887 on the approaching centenary of British settlement and what it meant to Indigenous Australians.

'The first land sale.' In this cartoon, the only people not allowed at the land auction in Melbourne in 1835 were the actual owners. (*Melbourne Punch*, 1855)

to react as they did; they felt the 'natives' were guilty of senseless violence and so they hit back in turn. The Europeans often thought they were punishing aggressors, forgetting or not realizing that they themselves had been the original aggressors in taking others' land.

Only in the 1960s did Aborigines' demands for both the return of some land and compensation for other land start to be widely heard, though they had been attempting to be heard for many years before then. By the 1970s, the justice of these demands was widely recognized by white Australians and governments. The Commonwealth and South Australian governments moved first to grant land rights; the Queensland and Western Australian governments were particularly reluctant to grant freehold title; in New South Wales and Victoria, intentions were better but results meagre until the 1980s. The Mabo case in 1992 and the Wik case in 1996 finally recognized that there was such a thing as 'native title [ownership]' in land.

From the beginning of their contact, misunderstanding and ignorance, though often combined with good intentions, long prevented white Australians from working out a satisfactory relationship with Aborigines. The considerable unrest from the 1970s to the 2000s was largely the product of a past accepted passively by most Australians but remembered bitterly by Aborigines. 'White Australia,' they said in 1988, 'has a black history.'

History
Until the 1960s, most Australian historians and writers of textbooks had virtually ignored the place of the Aborigines in Australian history. One writer commented that they had become a mere 'melancholy footnote' in Australian history. Historians have since recognized that the Aborigines at various times and in various places have been a significant influence in the evolution of Australian society and also that the history of the Indigenous people is important to study for its own sake. Knowledge of the history of past race relations also helps people understand the present state of affairs. Aboriginal reactions to white settlement were found to be as worthy of study, and as interesting,

as are those of Maoris, Zulus and Comanches. The availability of sources and the ability of scholars to be empathic about different cultures have both improved greatly in the last forty years. One reason is that, since the 1970s, Aboriginal people themselves have increasingly been collecting and publishing the stories that constitute their history, and researching and writing about their people's experiences and teaching other Australians about Aboriginal history in schools and universities.

Marcia Langton, a leading Aboriginal historian and foundation Professor of Indigenous Studies at the University of Melbourne from 2000.

It needs to be acknowledged that most of the written sources for Aboriginal history are still in fact 'white' in origin. The reliability and interpretations of Aboriginal oral traditions are also contested. Because all history is selective, although the author has attempted to be as even-handed as possible, bias is inevitable.

FURTHER READING

Barlow, A., and M. Hill, *You and Me Living Together: The Story of Aboriginal Land Rights*, Melbourne: Heinemann Library, 2006.

Berry, B., and H.L. Tischler, *Race and Ethnic Relations*, 4th ed., Boston: Houghton Mifflin, 1978.

Curthoys, A., 'Indigenous Subjects', in D. Schreuder and S. Ward (eds), *Australia's Empire*, Melbourne: Oxford University Press, 2008, pp. 78–102.

Hercus, L., and P. Sutton (eds), *This Is What Happened: Historical Narratives by Aborigines*, Canberra: Australian Institute of Aboriginal Studies, 1986.

Samson, Jane, *Race and Empire*, Harlow, UK; New York: Pearson/ Longman, 2005.

Stanner, W.E.H., *After the Dreaming*, Sydney: ABC, 1968.

2 Before 1788

When there are two parties in a relationship, the background and character of each party will affect the nature of the relationship between them. The same sort of rule applies to relationships between groups: in other words, the unique background and character of the Aborigines affected the nature of their relations with the incoming white Australians, and vice versa. Hence, there is a need for a short preliminary discussion of the most important features of pre-contact Aboriginal society and way of life.

First, a word about the word, Aborigines. The word 'Aborigines' comes from the Latin *ab origine*, meaning 'from the beginning'. It was originally applied by Europeans to the indigenous people of any land they encountered but, for the want of any obvious alternative common term, has come to be the accepted name especially for Australia's indigenous people. They had, after all, been the only people on the continent for over 40,000 years. Nevertheless, 'Aborigines' is in a sense an indigenous identity artificially constructed by outsiders, not originally a term of self-description by a people who had no consciousness of themselves as one, distinct people. This awareness only occurred after aliens arrived in their country. There were as many as 600 different language and culture groups before 1788.

Aboriginal lifestyles and Aboriginal experiences do not comprise a series of separate compartments labelled economy, society, culture, religion, and so on. It is important to realize that all features of Aboriginal life were closely interwoven in a complicated interdependence, quite unlike our modern, Western society. It is also important to note that all cultures change over time. This applies to both pre-contact and post-contact Aboriginal societies, although change was far faster after contact. What is an authentic Aboriginal culture is not just the pre-contact or 'traditional' one.

Their Origins

Every group of Aboriginal people had stories about their origins and history. These stories linked past with present, and linked the people with the landscape and with different plants and creatures. The creation of all things happened in a time called the Dreaming. The Dreaming was not just 'a long time ago' but is eternally present through the re-telling of the stories of past events in story, song and dance. Life was a cycle: people and nature were continually dying and being reborn or renewed.

Dreaming stories about the origins of their ancestors gave, broadly

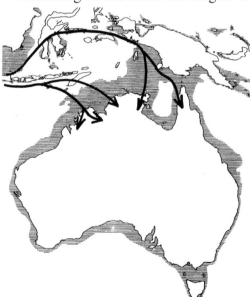

speaking, two different origins. In the stories told by many communities of Aborigines, their ancestors were created in Australia. People and other living things were created out of the land and along with it. In the stories of some other groups, however, their spirit-ancestors came over the sea from the north in canoes.

Map 1: Australia, showing the coastline during the last ice age and possible routes for human settlement about 50,000 years ago.

Generally, all communities had stories which depicted creative spirit beings moving about the landscape along particular paths creating natural features. In the Aboriginal Dreaming stories, people turned into rocks, mountains and islands or animals and birds turned into people, frogs brought rain. The stories were sung along the paths followed by the spirit beings. One creative spirit being was the Rainbow Serpent, which features in stories in many places, and created waterways such as rivers and waterholes and ended up in the sea. Small replicas of the Rainbow Serpent remained: the carpet snake, a python with a colourful pattern on its back.

Lake Mungo in 2000, showing the 'Walls of China', near where the earliest human remains in Australia were found in the 1960s. In 40,000 BP, the lake was full of water and teeming with life to support human settlement.

Aboriginal Society

Contrary to the belief of the first white observers, Aboriginal groups did have definite ties with particular pieces of land. They were not complete nomads, but rather semi-nomadic: that is, they camped at different temporary campsites within their own identifiable territory.

Though the tie with the territory was not obvious to the European eye, it was in fact stronger than the same tie in Western society.

The Aboriginal group and, indeed, the individual Aboriginal, was tied to their homeland in both physical and spiritual ways. Each Aboriginal person was part of the life-cycle of nature. They believed in the existence of the spirit-world, from which they were born and to which they would return when they died.

The wellbeing of the flora and fauna and that of the Aboriginal group were linked: prosperity for one meant prosperity for the other. This was practical: for example, flourishing kangaroos meant better food supplies for the Aborigines but the killing of too many kangaroos was, in the long run, not good for the Aborigines. They also systematically burned undergrowth to keep their hunting grounds clear and stimulate regrowth of feed for their prey. By these and other methods, they controlled and conserved their natural environment. The religious side of the interdependence involved Aborigines in corroborees which were 'increase rites' intended to encourage the growth of food sources and the wellbeing of nature.

Aborigines were hunters and gatherers. They had no agriculture and led a semi-nomadic life, each clan or band within its own territory. Only the Torres Strait islanders had gardens, although some Aboriginal groups had fish traps or encouraged certain food plants to grow. Each band moved around according to seasonal variations in the availability of food. The kinds of foods varied according to climate and environment.

Tribes, individual Aborigines and certain sub-groups (such as women, 'sections', generations) were related spiritually to sacred sites and species of fish, animals, plants, and so on. The particular thing was one's 'totem' and one had to protect it and it would protect the person. Since both the spiritual and material wellbeing of an Aboriginal group depended on relationships with sites spread around a particular identifiable territory, it is quite wrong to deny that land belonged to the Aborigines — or, rather, that they belonged to the land.

Early European observers were of the opinion that the Aborigines had no social, political and military organization to speak of. Unlike the North American Indians and the Maori, they were not organized into fairly large tribes with readily identifiable leaders and a capacity for organized warfare on a big scale. There were about 600 distinct languages spoken; each language grouping tends to be called a 'tribe', but it lacked any overall political structure or chief. (See Map 2.) The language groups were divided in local clans or hordes. An Aboriginal tribe was not an organized body at all; 'tribe' is merely a convenient term to describe a number of 'clans' or 'hordes' or 'bands' (anthropologists' terms) who spoke the same language and had much in common in their social organization and customs and who regarded each other as closer relatives than more distant clans or bands. The tribes had no common leadership and hardly ever (if at all) gathered together, though they would intermarry and trade amongst themselves. A large tribe had around 1500 members; a clan varied in size from less than 50 to over 200, according to available resources. In richer and more productive areas, such as coastal river valleys, the population was denser.

For a long time, it was widely accepted that the total Aboriginal population in 1788 was around 300,000. Recent research and investigation has led to the acceptance of the strong likelihood that there were between 500,000 and 850,000 people living in Australia before the Europeans arrived. The population density was greatest in the most fertile areas in river valleys and on coastlines in warmer climates. But even the harshest desert areas were inhabited. The density ranged from one person per 8 square kilometres to one person per 100 square kilometres.

The most significant unit of society was the smaller clan or band. Each band or clan had it own territory and each territory had its own dreaming stories. The older men and women had to teach the young all the stories and law so they could become full adults. Though it did not have one dominant chief, it was governed by immemorial tradition, interpreted by the older men and, in fact, had a complex and tightly knit social structure. The older men governed the clan. Sorcery was

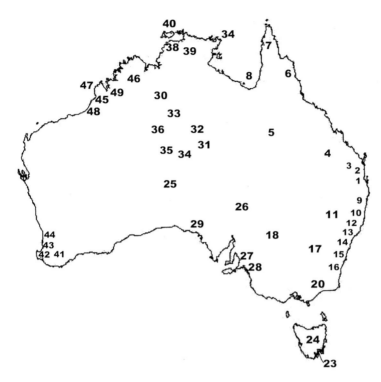

Map 2: Australia, showing the approximate locations of 49 of the approximately 600 'tribes' (or 'language groups' or 'nations') occupying Australia in 1788.

Queensland
1 Yuggera
2 Gubbi Gubbi/Badtjala
3 Wakka Wakka
4 Jiman
5 Kalkadoons
6 Guugu-Yimidhirr
7 Wik
8 Lardil/Kaiadilt

New South Wales
9 Bandjalang
10 Gumbainggar
11 Gamilaroi
12 Dhangati
13 Biripi
14 Dharug/Eora
15 Dharawal
16 Yuin
17 Wiradjuri
18 Barkindji

Victoria
19 Kulin
20 Kurnai
21 Yorta Yorta
22 Tjapwurong

Tasmania
23 Nuenonne
24 Lairmairrener (Big River)

South Australia
25 Pitjantjatjara
26 Dieri
27 Kaurna
28 Ngarrindjeri
29 Wirangu

Northern Territory
30 Gurindji
31 Aranda

32 Anmatyerre
33 Walbiri
34 Yolngu
35 Luritja
36 Bibdubi
37 Jawoyn
38 Larrakia
39 Gagadju
40 Tiwi

Western Australia
41 Nyungar
42 Bibbulman
43 Pinjarup
44 Whadjuk
45 Karadjeri
46 Ngarrinyin
47 Nyul Nyul
48 Bardi
49 Worora

practised by the 'clever man', who could use magic stones. It was believed that they could 'sing' someone to death.

Aboriginal men shown fishing in bark canoes.

Everyone had a place, and everyone was related to everyone else, at least in the clan, and in theory to anyone with whom he would come into contact in the course of his life. This was the case because all members of a tribe could claim to trace their ancestry to a common 'dreaming' ancestor. And it was important because a person was defined — and his behaviour determined — by his or her relationships. There were very definite rules about how one had to treat one's mother-in-law, grandfather, and so on. One particularly important aspect of this was that very rigid rules governed who might marry whom, and any deviation could (and often did) result in fatal consequences.

An inter-tribal confrontation sketched by Victorian Koori, Tommy McCrae, about 1880. McCrae was recollecting an earlier time, before the whites came, when such conflict was common but controlled.

Because an Aboriginal person usually married outside his or her clan, though within the tribe, the web of relations spread very wide. When white people were encountered, it tested Aboriginal ingenuity to find a place for them in their complex system of social relations. But they often did just that, incorporating significant whitefellas, such as grazier-employers, in the web of kinship obligations.

To add to the complications, most tribes were also divided for social and ceremonial purposes into two 'moieties', or four 'sections', or even sometimes into eight 'sub-sections' with complex rules governing whom one could marry. The 'extended family' of aunts and uncles and grandparents was, and continues to be, important.

On the whole, tribes and even clans or bands within a tribe kept to their own territory. Certain valuable things (for example, quartz, ochre, shells) were traded from tribe to tribe over vast distances. Sometimes there would be marriages between different tribes, though generally people married within the one language group. In some areas during a particular season, there would be huge resources of food, which the

Cave paintings in Mutawintji National Park, in far western New South Wales, photographed in 2000.

local tribe would allow others to come and share for a limited period — for example, bunya nuts in south-east Queensland in February, Bogong moths in the Australian Alps in September, fish in many river and coastal locations. These times were also used to hold celebrations of song and dance ('corroborees'), to trade and to arrange marriages.

Closely interdependent with nature and with their fellows, the Aborigines lived in a world in which they knew their places and were in turn known. Traditionally, they associated the wellbeing of particular animals and plants with the wellbeing of particular people. The rhythm of life, in nature and in human society, was orderly and regular, even if not easy. A person went through the cycle of spirit-birth–birth–initiation–marriage–death–rebirth, nature went through

Wurlies near Ernabella in 1958, housing for some of the Pitjantjatjara people in north-western South Australia. The Presbyterian mission interfered little with traditional life. (Photograph by Hamilton Aiken)

its endless cycle with social life adapted to nature. Aboriginal society was geared to the routine. It was finely tuned so that maximum result could be obtained (for example, in food gathering) with an economy of effort. And every experience and every member of that society had a known place.

What, then, would Aborigines do when confronted with people and experiences without a known place? What behaviour would be appropriate when they were faced with something totally beyond past experience and wisdom? This was one of the dilemmas presented to the Aborigines by the coming of the Europeans.

The resistance offered to white intruders in Asia, America, Africa and the Pacific gave those intruders cause to respect their opponents. The Aborigines lacked two things which made effective defence possible: developed technology and the capacity for large-scale organized warfare. The Aboriginal tool and weapon kit depended on stone, bone and wood. Though much finely wrought stone weaponry was produced, it was not highly developed to form permanent arsenals. It is also believed that, in the 200 years before white contact, the level of stone-working skill declined in many parts of south-eastern Australia, and bone and wood were being used to a greater degree for weapons and tools.

We have already seen how complex and interrelated Aboriginal society was and also the fact that the clan was the largest effective unit of society. The tribe was a mere 'linguistic expression', and many tribes and even clans were mutually hostile. There were often small wars between neighbours, usually over law-breaking not over land. Large-scale warfare was obviously out of the question for organizational reasons. It is worth noting in passing that some of the significant causes of war in Western society, such as greed for land and goods, were virtually non-existent; thus there was less reason to build up a large-scale capacity for wars. Where there were hostilities they were on a small scale and most often arose from an argument over a woman or a death.

Prehistory

It should not be assumed that Aboriginal society was totally unchanging before 1788. Archaeologists have been able to discern considerable changes in Aboriginal technology over the centuries. Tools and other items had been successively refined — not necessarily 'improved' by European standards, but better adapted to the environment and the needs of the users. Apart from adaptation, contact with other cultures could lead to changes, particularly on the northern coast.

Adaptation, not confrontation, was the keynote of Aboriginal life. Anthropologists and archaeologists have been able to discern social change, as well. At different times, climatic change, giant marsupials, floods and volcanic activity challenged and modified the Aboriginal way of life.

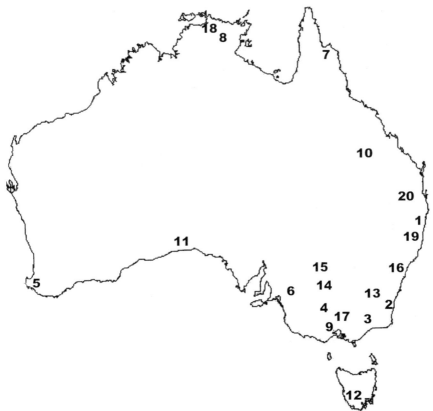

Map 3: Australia, showing significant archaeological sites. Lake Mungo (14) and Kow Swamp (4) have been involved in debates about whether there was more than one founding 'race' in early Australia.

1 Ballina
2 Burrill Lake
3 Cloggs Cave
4 Cohuna, Coobool Creek
  and Kow Swamp
5 Devil's Lair
6 Devon Downs, Fromm's Landing
7 Early Man

8 Ingaladdi
9 Keilor, Lancefield
10 Kenniff Cave
11 Koonalda Cave
12 Kutikina Cave
13 Lake George
14 Lake Mungo

15 Lake Nitchie
16 Lapstone Creek
17 Mount William
18 Oenpelli
19 Seelands
20 Talgai

Aborigines using fire to hunt kangaroos, in a painting by Joseph Lycett (1820).

Fire was the most important tool used by the Aborigines: in cooking and tool-making and to modify and conserve their environment. It was used in clearing undergrowth to help hunting and make travel easier. It encouraged the spread of fire-tolerant plants and new growth liked by grazing marsupials. Regular, smaller fires prevented catastrophic fires. The use of fire contributed to the 'parkland' appearance of many parts of the landscape when white men arrived. But it probably also destroyed feed eaten by certain megafauna (large animals) and contributed to their extinction. It also denuded hillsides and river banks of vegetation, which led to increased run-off, erosion and even desertification.

An artist's impression of a diprotodon, an example of a large marsupial which became extinct after the arrival of human beings.

The biggest change in the environment which faced Aborigines was the ending of the last ice age and the resulting rise of sea levels between 15,000 and 8000 years ago. This cut Tasmania off from the mainland. Another change was the extinction of megafauna (such as diprotodons and marsupial tigers) about 15,000 years ago, which may have been the result of hunting by the Aborigines. About 5000 years ago, the dingo came and caused the thylacine (Tasmanian tiger) and Tasmanian devil to become extinct on the mainland. The thylacine and Tasmanian devil remained in Tasmania because dingoes arrived in Australia after the sea level rose and Tasmania was cut off. The isolation of the Tasmanians also led to significant differences of culture: they did not have boomerangs, would not eat scaled fish and had lost the art of making fire and had to carry fire-sticks.

It would seem that people have been in Australia for between 50,000 and 40,000 years. Understandably, they were isolated from much outside contact. Before the Europeans, the most extensive and intensive contact with outsiders occurred on the Arnhem Land coast from at least the 1720s to 1906. Macassans and Bugis (from what is now Indonesia) made annual visits to catch the trepang (or sea-slug or sea-cucumber), which they traded with Chinese merchants. Between 30 and 60 praus came every season, carrying about 30 men on each. The Aborigines learned much from these foreigners but certainly did not encourage them to settle. Mostly, the Aborigines were interested in only the material products of Macassan culture: dugout canoes, glass and metal, harpoons, rice and fruit, and tobacco. The trepangers also left behind tamarind trees, added words to the language and influenced burial customs. They also introduced smoking and smallpox. The influences were very localized except for smallpox, which spread across the continent.

It was not necessary, however, for direct contact to take place for Aboriginal culture to be influenced, as ideas and techniques could be (and were) gradually diffused over the centuries, particularly from Torres Strait. Extensive trading networks and seasonal feasting trips helped new ideas to spread.

A Macassan sailing vessel (prau).

It is important to remember that considerable variations existed between parts of Australia with regard to population density, diet and clothing — the result of the vast differences in natural environment. For example, in colder climates, furs were worn (except in Tasmania where grease was used instead). It followed that implements, customs and languages also varied greatly. For example, in harsh environments, marriage rules were more flexible and ritual less elaborate. Most changes and regional differences came about by diffusion of influences rather than invention, and by gradual adaptation rather than by rapid change.

Though there had been sporadic contact with a handful of mainly Dutch navigators, nothing had prepared the Aborigines for the sudden influx and spread of Europeans after 1788. Cook had sailed up the fertile east coast of Australia in 1770, having little contact with Aborigines until the *Endeavour* was beached near the present town of Cooktown. Sixteen years later, the British government, faced with over-crowded gaols and with little thought for the Aboriginal people, decided on a convict settlement at Botany Bay. The first 'Australia Day', 26 January 1788, a day for white Australians to celebrate but a melancholy one for black Australians, saw Governor Arthur Phillip landing at Sydney Cove.

FURTHER READING

On Aboriginal culture:
Berndt, R.M., and C.H. Berndt, *The First Australians*, Sydney: Ure Smith, 1967.
Edwards, W.H., *An Introduction to Aboriginal Societies*, 2nd ed., Tuggerah, NSW: Social Science Press, 2004.
Maddock, K.J., *The Australian Aborigines: A Portrait of Their Society*, Melbourne: Penguin, 1974.

On Australian prehistory:
Blainey, G.N., *The Triumph of the Nomads: A History of Ancient Australia*, Melbourne: Macmillan, 1975.
Flood, J.M., *Archaeology of the Dreamtime: The Story of Prehistoric Australia and its People*, rev. ed., Marleston, SA: J.B. Publishing, 2004.

PART ONE
Aboriginal Reactions to the Europeans

3   First Contacts

Aboriginal people reacted in a great variety of ways to their first encounter with the strangers. In some cases, clans had had contact with outsiders before, or had heard news about the strange beings — news which had spread a long distance from clan to clan and which prepared them somewhat for their first encounter. On the other hand, those with no expectations whatever were sometimes indifferent, as if the 'new thing' did not exist or perhaps was literally unbelievable and therefore could not exist. Or they could be paralysed with fear, run away terrified or even experience involuntary urination. Their reactions had much in common with universal human responses to a literally 'awesome' event. In the period of first contact, though, the most common reactions could be classified as avoidance or cautious approach, or a combination of both: avoidance shortly followed by approach, perhaps. Alternatively, avoidance and curiosity could be followed by hostility, verbal or physical.

Avoidance
The very first contact was between Wik people of western Cape York and Dutch sailors on the *Duyfken* in 1606. It seems that things went well for a while but ended in killings on both sides for reasons unknown. The first white men to contact particular Aboriginal groups, however, often noticed that the Aborigines tended to hide, be shy and avoid

A replica of the Dutch vessel *Duyfken*, which carried the first Europeans to make contact with Aborigines in 1606.

The *Endeavour*, commanded by Lieutenant James Cook, sailed close to the east coast in 1770, landing several times.. This 'floating island' was frequently ignored. (A nineteenth-century sketch)

contact. In particular, women and children were hidden away even if the men approached. Dampier noticed this in the north-west in 1688.

A couple of times in 1770, Cook's *Endeavour* was sailing up the east coast and passed close enough to shore to be easily seen by groups of Aborigines. Joseph Banks noticed that they 'were totally unmoved by … so remarkable an object as a ship must necessarily be to people who have never seen one'. When Cook was ashore at the Endeavour River (Cooktown, north Queensland) later that year, it took him a month to establish contact with the local Guugu Yimidhirr people. Governor Phillip took about four months in 1788 to make contact with Sydney's Aborigines, and finally had to resort to kidnapping Arabanoo at Manly on the last day of that year. Unfortunately, Arabanoo died of smallpox in May 1789.

Although in April 1789 two children had been found — a boy called Nanbarry aged nine or ten and a girl called Abaroo aged about fourteen — both suffering from smallpox, and had been cared for, it was decided to capture adults. After much effort, an expedition to Manly in November captured two men: Coleby aged about 35 and Bennelong aged about 25. Neither was eager to remain in captivity and

Bennelong, celebrated here as a Westernized gentleman and as a warrior, became (unwillingly at first) a go-between at Sydney Cove in 1789.

Coleby, apparently a man of authority, escaped within three weeks. The younger man enjoyed himself for a while, and escaped in May 1790.

In 1799, when Matthew Flinders landed at the mouth of the Clarence River to investigate a camp, he found it newly deserted. In 1822, when Captain John Bingle landed opposite Bribie Island (Queensland), he described the Aborigines there as extremely shy and guessed that they had never seen white men. John McDouall Stuart's party came upon a group of Aborigines in the north of the Northern Territory in June 1862; they 'set up a fearful yelling and squalling', and ran off as fast as they could. In Central Australia, the Western Aranda proved very difficult to contact. Though hundreds of white men had passed through the territories of their kinsfolk, the Northern, Southern and Central Aranda between 1872 and 1877, the Western Aranda steadfastly avoided contact with whites. Finally, when the Lutherans' Hermannsburg Mission was founded in their territory in 1877, they avoided it for two months.

An example of avoidance, about 1860, at Mount Kingston in the Northern Territory. A sketch by G.F. Angas of an incident in an expedition of John McDouall Stuart.

Causes

This kind of behaviour led to a fairly persistent belief amongst white people that Aborigines were timid or cowardly. (It was also occasionally said that they were treacherous and violent, but no one seemed to notice the contradiction). There were better reasons for the Aborigines' avoidance of contact with white men. In some cases, no doubt, avoidance can be explained by the fact that the Aboriginal group had heard stories on the grapevine about the brutality of white men elsewhere. This was certainly a policy decision on the part of the Aborigines, not just a case of natural shyness. But there are two more important reasons, arising from the Aboriginal way of life, which are similar and related to each other.

Firstly, underlying an apparent fear of the unexpected was the fact that Aboriginal society had no social or political machinery to deal with something completely new. As we have seen, Aboriginal society was one of routine, and geared to the regular rhythm of life and nature. While it coped smoothly with all the normal demands of life, a completely unheard-of emergency naturally caught the Aborigines unprepared. They rarely met strangers, and these strangers looked very strange indeed and did not seem to know the rules or how to approach them in the appropriate manner. No such thing as temporary or emergency plans for a particular purpose existed. A society with strong leadership at the top is often better placed to react positively. On the other hand, it does seem that some (or possibly most) clans had an established protocol for meeting strangers, which involved politely ignoring them at first. To be inquisitive was seen to be rude.

Secondly, if Aboriginal society was not tuned to respond to the unexpected and tended, therefore, to avoid it when it came, it is not surprising that some Aborigines thought that the white people were not in fact real but illusions or evil spirits which would go away if ignored. There is some interesting evidence for this. Of course, Aborigines believed in spirit-beings, legendary heroes and rebirths, so this kind of reaction would be understandable. Apart from that, some of the terms used to describe white people are very suggestive. For instance, 'gubba', which is still in common use in parts of south-eastern Australia, means 'ghost'. Some Aborigines had been heard to express the belief that after they died they would 'jump up' (be resurrected) as white men. This particular idea may have origins apart from traditional religious belief. Some of the 'wild white men' who spent several years with Aborigines, such as William Buckley in the Port Phillip area (later Victoria), were 'recognized' by them as dead friends and named after them. Members of the Galibal, a clan on the far north coast of New South Wales, sometimes disparagingly refer to white men as 'dugai' meaning corpse or, literally, 'stinking white flesh'.

Cautiously Approaching the White Man

Eventually, of course, each Aboriginal group had to come to terms in some way with the white invader. Often, the first step was what Professor A.P. Elkin called 'tentative approach'. Curiosity was not a marked characteristic of Aborigines in normal circumstances (it was often regarded as rude), but these were not normal circumstances. Gradually, a newly contacted Aboriginal group would itself offer contact, perhaps firstly with two or three armed men, then later with a larger group and eventually with women and children as well. Particularly if the white men seemed intent on staying but were not being too difficult, a reconnaissance such as this 'tentative approach' was a sensible first step towards exploiting a peculiar situation. Often, groups had heard of the white men in advance, as news passed along trade routes.

At the very beginning, around Sydney, there was an equally sudden change from avoidance to approach; however, Governor Phillip had to wait for two years for it to happen. Early contacts showed the puzzlement of the Dharug about the sex of the newcomers, considering that the men were clean-shaven and covered by clothing. In one incident, a soldier was ordered to pull down his breeches to prove the manhood of white men. Something similar tended to happen quite widely over Australia. Sometimes Aborigines came in from considerable distances to white settlements.

When Captain Bingle landed opposite Bribie Island in 1822 he found the Aborigines to be very shy. When he landed again the next day, he was overwhelmed with affection as the Aborigines hugged and made 'a great fuss' over him, giving him their weapons. Unlike Flinders twenty-three years before him in the same area, Bingle wisely allowed the Aborigines to take his three-cornered hat, and by his simple gesture avoided the trouble Flinders caused by being very possessive towards his hat. As a result, Bingle was able to maintain good relations with the Aborigines while he stayed. When he and his crew left, Bingle later wrote, 'the whole tribe were in great distress ... bewailing our departure'.

In what ways did Aborigines expect an approach to white society to help them? With the explorers, one probable motive in helping them was to encourage them to keep going and leave the territory. Another important motive was to benefit from the Europeans' superior technology. The tomahawk was greatly prized; its steel blade was keener than that of a stone axe and better for making shields from bark, for cutting possums out of logs and for skinning animals. Tobacco also quickly attracted the Aborigines, as did tea, sugar and flour. In South Australia in 1837, some Aborigines refused to take oatmeal instead of flour, prompting the remark that they 'wouldn't eat their porridge!' It seems to have taken longer for Aborigines to gain a taste for alcohol (see pp. 70 and 77).

A statue of Yagan in Perth, erected in 1984 and commemorating his role as 'chief of the Swan River'. After initially peaceful relations, conflict developed, a bounty was put on his head and he was killed in 1833.

It is important to realize, in fact, that Aboriginal people took what they needed or wanted, not simply what they were offered, be it oatmeal or education. White people had imposed themselves on the Aborigines but the latter were not passive victims. In return, Aborigines, would offer women, their own tools (useless to the Europeans) and goods, food, information about the land or even their labour. They often offered help to explorers, sometimes successfully, but foolishly proud responses to these offers from individual explorers could lead to tragedy. Frequently, they would attempt to incorporate settlers into their kinship network. This was not just a sentimental action but was also an attempt to create an obligation in their new-found relatives to share their goods.

Where contact was occasional or settlement sparse and the Aborigines did not feel particularly threatened, contact was tentative or guarded and reasonably friendly. Where the first Europeans were semi-itinerant workers with little impact on the environment, such as some types of timber-getters, this situation might last for more than a few months. However, the exceptions to the 'tentative approach' were so many and widespread that it would be wrong to think of it as the normal thing.

Some activities were perceived as greater threats than others and the clans reacted accordingly: farming and gold-mining were very destructive of the environment and the Europeans involved had little need of Aboriginal labour. Grazing had less environmental impact than some other white-man activities and the graziers needed Aboriginal labour, so squatters (early graziers) often invited and welcomed tentative approach rather than outright resistance.

FURTHER READING

Clendinnen, Inga, *Dancing with Strangers,* 2nd ed., Melbourne: Text Publishing, 2005.

Reynolds, Henry, *The Other Side of the Frontier: Aboriginal Resistance to the European Invasion of Australia,* Sydney: UNSW Press, 2006.

4   Resisting the Invaders

Many of us are familiar with the names Chief Sitting Bull, Crazy Horse, Geronimo and other Native American heroes. But how many of us have heard of the heroes of the Aboriginal resistance? Of men like Wil-le-me-ring, who speared Governor Phillip at Manly in 1790, or Pemulwuy, who led the resistance against the early settlers around Sydney in the 1790s, or 'Mosquito' and his mob in Tasmania in the 1820s, Windradyne (or 'Saturday') of the Wiradjuri around Bathurst, NSW, in the 1820s or 'Pigeon' (Jandamurra) in the Kimberleys of Western Australia in the 1890s? To be sure, the Aboriginal heroes did not last very long against the heavy odds, but the view that the Aborigines were wiped out because they offered no credible resistance is basically wrong. For instance, in the 1850s and 1860s pastoral expansion in western Queensland was held up for years in some areas by fierce Aboriginal resistance, such as by the Kalkadoons in the Cloncurry district. Considering the social and military disadvantages, Aboriginal people resisted intelligently and remarkably well.

Conciliation
However, there were exceptions to violent resistance and, before discussing the violence, we may notice briefly the exceptions. Violence was not inevitable. Where it did not break out, or was limited, the cause

was nearly always a conciliatory settler or missionary. If the local white settler sought peace and was prepared to give something to the Aborigines in return for use of land, something they thought valuable (for example, access to wild animals or water, regular rations, clothing, medical help, some freedom to wander the area unmolested, or perhaps protection against less sympathetic white men or the Native Police), then violence could be largely avoided. Sometimes, by employing Aborigines, the settler could provide a degree of compensation for the collapse of their economy. But this collapse, as it came mainly from the disastrous environmental effects of the Europeans' economic activities, was irreversible and eventually total in area after area.

Some paternalistic or conciliatory settlers who were able to avert violence are not as well known as they deserve to be. While other settlers were suffering raids in the 1820s, the Suttor family of Bathurst had a peaceful relationship with Windradyne and his people. In the 1820s and 1830s, Alexander Berry was a very large landowner in the Shoalhaven valley on the south coast of New South Wales. Berry took fatherly care of the physical needs of 'his natives' and employed them on his estates. His brother, David, supervised the education of the children of Aborigines and of convict workers. In the middle of the century, the Everett brothers of Ollera in northern New England achieved an excellent understanding with the local Aborigines, learned their language, employed them successfully and encouraged them to remain on their sheep station. Tom Petrie, one of the pioneers of early Queensland, was well known for acting in the interests of Aborigines. Later in the nineteenth century, Robert Christison of Lammermoor in Queensland was equally benevolent and avoided clashes. He was reported to have said to one of his black employees, 'Very good, Barney. Country belonging to you; sheep belonging to me.'

On the upper Clarence River on the north coast of New South Wales one squatter, Edward Ogilvie, had virtually a treaty from 1842 with the local clan in whose territory his Yulgilbar station was located (see Reading 16). Native animals (and wild honey!), access to water, clothing, rations and, later in the century, housing and schooling were guaranteed to the Aborigines in return for use of the land for sheep and cattle. As the land was everything to them, this was an unequal bargain, but it was probably the best the Aborigines could expect in the circumstances. Ogilvie employed them extensively, especially during the gold rushes, spoke their language well, had wrestling matches with them and generally promoted friendly relations, with the result that the local clan was preserved intact longer than almost any other in New South Wales. Sometimes, however, paternalism could cruelly mock proud people; for example, sometimes army-style bronze 'king-plates' were placed around the necks of tribal 'leaders'.

Many Aboriginal 'leaders' were recognized as 'chiefs' by governors, settlers and others. This king-plate comes from the upper Clarence River in northern New South Wales, where squatter Edward Ogilvie and Toolbillibam had worked out an agreement to share the land in 1842. (See Reading 16 below, p. 124.)

A few white men, usually escaped convicts, joined Aboriginal clans and could act as translators and go-betweens for the Aborigines and settlers and sought to foster good relations. These 'wild white men' included William Buckley, who spent from 1803 to 1835 with the Wathaurong in Victoria; James 'Duramboi' Davis, who spent 1829 to 1842 with various tribes in south-east Queensland; and Richard Craig, who spent some time on the north coast of New South Wales in the late 1820s.

Missionaries, too, aimed to promote peace and often found themselves defending Aborigines against white 'realists' who thought Aborigines less than human and who rode rough-shod over their interests and lives. Lancelot Threlkeld, in conducting his Lake Macquarie mission to the Awabagal tribe from 1825 to 1841, learned the Awabagal tongue and began to translate the gospels with the help of his Awabagal friend, Biraban. The mission broke up when most of the tribe had died out or drifted to Newcastle and Sydney, but Threlkeld later (when seamen's chaplain in Sydney) often appeared in

William Buckley, a 'wild white man', an escaped convict who lived with Port Phillip Aborigines for 32 years.

court on behalf of Awabagal people or other Aborigines, as translator or character witness. The missionaries at Hermannsburg in Central Australia from the 1870s pursued a similar policy of constructive conciliation and mutual respect, with benefit for both sides.

Violent and Non-Violent Resistance

Despite the efforts of some enlightened settlers, officials and missionaries, violence between white and black was common, and lasted in northern and central Australia until the 1930s. White settlers could give excuses for their takeover of Aboriginal territory: after all, it was clear to them that the Aborigines were not using the land. Where there was no effort by whites even to share land, Aboriginal

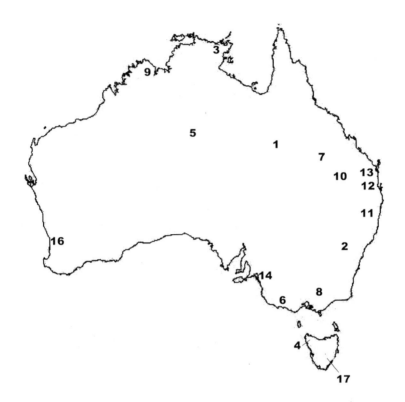

Map 4: Australia, showing the locations of some massacres and battles.

1 Battle Mountain	6 Convincing Ground	12 Kilcoy
2 Bathurst & Bells Falls Gorge	7 Cullin-la-ringo	13 Manumbar
	8 Faithfull/ Benalla	14 Maria
3 Caledon Bay	9 Forrest River	15 Myall Creek
4 Cape Grim	10 Hornet Bank	16 Pinjarra
5 Coniston	11 Kangaroo Creek	17 Risdon Cove

resistance was to be expected. This resistance was at its height, over
the whole length of south-eastern Australia, in the 1830s and 1840s,
when the frontier was being extended very rapidly everywhere. Before
this, clashes were fairly widespread, but scattered and minor, caused
by such things as abuse of Aboriginal women, refusal to pay back
favours, desecration of totem sites or simple lack of effort by whites

to communicate. Aboriginal resistance was so intense in the 1830–48 period that one observer referred to a 'black war' on the frontier. Though this term well describes the intensity of the resistance, it is misleading as the resistance was not in any way organized, except on a very local basis. Aborigines resisted until overcome by arms or weight of numbers or until they were uneasily included in the Europeans' economy.

The type of resistance offered in this period, more systematic and 'intelligent' than before, has been described as a form of guerrilla warfare. The intensity and time span of resistance depended on several factors: the density of the Aboriginal population; the rate and density of European settlement and resulting environmental impact; the terrain and vegetation which might provide cover or safer bases; and the type of stock in the area (sheep being more destructive than cattle in most respects).

Certain areas were notable for this strung-out, small-scale guerrilla resistance. Often they were in or near rugged, mountainous or heavily wooded areas. Examples included the Hawkesbury River area, the Bathurst district, western Tasmania, the eastern falls of New England, south-eastern Queensland and north-eastern New South Wales, the scrub of the lower Murray River, the Cloncurry area of Queensland and the Kimberleys of Western Australia. In the last case, in the 1890s, Jandamara turned from police helper to freedom-fighter and became one of the few resistance fighters to use guns. The bloodiest clashes occurred in Queensland from the 1860s; Victoria witnessed

'A Native Chief of Bathurst', an illustration in a book published in 1820. It is likely that this is Windradyne, a leader of Wiradjuri resistance around 1824–25.

probably the least violence. This was partly because of the Native Mounted Police and the fact that the Queensland frontier was later, by which time the technology of guns had improved. One of the last incidents was the Coniston massacre in central Australia in 1928, a police-led revenge raid for a relatively trivial act of Aboriginal violence. Although the overall death toll of resistance and conflict has been the subject of intense scholarly research and debate, it is has generally been estimated at about 2000 whites and up to 20,000 Aborigines, covering approximately the first 150 years of settlement.

An example of resistance in 1861 at Bulloo in south-western Queensland, in a painting by W.O. Hodgkinson.

Sometimes, unlike traditional Aboriginal warfare, the resistance might have had a particular leader, and the 'guerrilla force' may have consisted only of the young men. Typically, a band of young men would take to the hills, and sweep down and kill stock when the squatter's attention was elsewhere. The dead sheep or cattle were not always for food, because the men would sometimes kill hundreds at a time.

It is, however, important not to over-estimate the degree of violent

Hornet Bank station homestead in central Queensland, the site of a bloody retaliation by the Yiman people in 1857 for mistreatment of their women by white settlers. Eleven were killed and the women were raped. Retaliation against them was far more bloody.

resistance in reaction against the former tendency of white Australians to pretend it did not happen at all. There were many forms of resistance, and not all were violent. One of the most interesting forms of non-violent resistance was the use of sorcery to repel the whites or to punish other Aborigines who may have helped whites. 'Clever men' attempted to counter firearms with magic and, years later, Aborigines told stories of the successful magic.

Only temporary success was obtained in checking the advancing frontier. To make matters worse, the European invasion indirectly increased inter-tribal violence. Violent resistance was always put down in the end, but resistance continued in more subtle ways. To all intents and purposes, the Aborigines were soon a conquered people.

READING I

Aboriginal Resistance
Thomas Bartlett and a number of other mid-nineteenth-century observers were under no illusions as to the causes of inter-racial violence.

It must not be forgotten, while we are meditating on the treatment of natives of New Holland, that their country is occupied by force — that they attempted, but in vain, to beat off the English settlers. However much this question may be mystified, it is evident that New Holland is only held by the right of might. Therefore, it is not justifiable to assert that all the evils which have been brought on the Aborigines by the settlement of the whites in their country, have arisen from the inherent depravity of their natures; for they took their origin from the system which has been pursued in regard to colonies, aggravated, however, there can be no doubt, by the description of persons [i.e. convicts], who formed a large — and almost the only working — population among the early settlers in the oldest of these colonies.

T. Bartlett, *New Holland: Its Colonization, Productions and Resources*,
London, 1843, pp. 78-79.

READING 2

Aboriginal Resistance

There were many notable massacres of blacks by whites and vice versa. Following is an account of the Risdon Cove incident in Tasmania in 1804.

Lieutenant Moore to Lieutenant-Governor Collins,
Risdon Cove, 7th May 1804
Sir,
        Agreeable to your desire I have the honour of acquainting you with the Circumstances that led to the attack on the Natives, which you will perceive was the consequence of their own hostile Appearance.
    It would appear from the numbers of them and the Spears, etc., with which they were armed, that their design was to attack us, however, it was not till they had thoroughly convinced me of their Intentions by using violence to a Settler's wife and my own Servant who was returning into Camp with some Kangaroos. One of which they took from him, that they were fired upon on their coming into Camp, and Surrounding it.
    I went towards them with five Soldiers, their appearance and numbers

I thought very far from friendly; during this time I was informed that a party of them was beating Birt, the Settler, at his farm. I then dispatched Two Soldiers to his assistance, with orders not to fire if they could avoid it; however, they found it necessary, and one was killed on the Spot, and another was found Dead in the Valley.

But at this time a great party was in Camp, and on a proposal from Mr Mountgarrett to fire one of the Carronades to intimidate them they dispersed.

Mr Mountgarrett with Some Soldiers and Prisoners followed them Some distance up the Valley, and had reason to Suppose more were wounded, as one was seen to be taken away bleeding; during the Time they were in Camp a number of old men were perceived at the foot of the Hill near the Valley employed in preparing spears.

I have now Sir, as near as I can recollect given you the leading particulars and hope there has nothing been done but what you approve of.

I have etc.,

Willm. Moore, Lieut: N.S.W. Corps.

Enclosure No. 1, Despatch from Lieutenant-Governor David Collins to Governor of New South Wales, P.G. King, 15 May 1804, in *Historical Records of Australia*, Series III, Vol. I, pp. 242–43.

READING 3

Aboriginal Resistance
From 1839 the Commissioners of Crown Lands in New South Wales were part-time protectors of the Aborigines, and they reported to the Colonial Secretary annually. The following report from the Clarence River district gives cases of Aboriginal resistance.

Commissioner of Crown Lands
Office, Clarence River,
6th January, 1846.

Sir,

In forwarding the Annual Report on the State of the aborigines in the District of Clarence River during the Year 1845, I regret the necessity of having to enumerate a series of outrages falling nothing short, either in number or atrocity, of the melancholy catalogue furnished in my report for the year 1844.

In the month of February, a Shepherd in the employ of Mr Archibald Boyd was murdered at that Gentleman's Station, on one of the Southern branches of the River Clarence, on which occasion between three and four hundred sheep were destroyed. In the month of March also, one of Messrs Mann and Hook's Shepherds was killed, and a flock of one Thousand sheep driven away from their Station, which is situated on the same stream as and within about thirty miles of Mr Boyd's; by far the greater portion of the sheep were destroyed, in consequence of the overseer's delaying to send information to the Police, until the flock had been several days in the possession of the Natives. This was an outrage of a peculiarly distressing nature, as the unfortunate man who was murdered had but recently arrived from England and left behind him a wife and two infant children.

One of the sheep stations of Messrs Bundock on the upper part of the Richmond River was twice attacked during the month of June; on the last occasion, the hut was plundered of all its contents, and the watchman dangerously speared in three several places. An Attack was also made in the same month on Mr McLean's Station, but no loss or injury was sustained. In addition to the above more heinous offences, a quantity of Cattle have been killed during the year on the respective runs of the following Gentlemen: – Mr Fawcett, Mr Irving, Mr Wyndham, Mr Eaton and Mr E. Hamilton.

As it affords reason to anticipate the discontinuance by the Natives in this locality of outrages, such as I have detailed, it is some satisfaction to me to be enabled to state that all the preceding depredations have been committed by the Tribes on the outskirts of the District, who have but recently come in contact with Europeans, and that nothing can be more peaceable than the disposition evinced by the Aboriginal inhabitants of the Interior and more settled portions of the District.

I have, etc.,
Oliver Fry

> *Historical Records of Australia*, Series I, Vol. XXV, pp. 4–5.

READING 4

Aboriginal Resistance

The Aborigines knew their land had been stolen, and believed they were entitled to compensation, even in the first half of the nineteenth century, as the following statement from an Aboriginal elder at Wollombi, NSW, shows:

> What we do, bail not fight like New Zealand fellow, no! I have land, and very hunger. No, did no bad, we got no blanket! What for?

> Quoted in New South Wales Legislative Council, *Votes and Proceedings*, 1845, p. 972.

QUESTIONS FOR READINGS I TO 4

How does each writer view the causes of conflict between Aborigines and Europeans? How did the causes vary? Why?

In each case, can blame be laid at the feet of particular persons or groups?

Was conflict inevitable?

FURTHER READING

Reynolds, Henry, *The Other Side of the Frontier: Aboriginal Resistance to the European Invasion of Australia,* Sydney: UNSW Press, 2006.

5 Adapting to a New Situation

The Aborigines were not simply parasitic on the white economy: often they were relied upon by that economy, particularly in remoter pastoral areas (and at one time all areas were remote and sparsely settled). Therefore, it is rather more accurate to say that the Aborigines 'accommodated' themselves to the new civilization. Like all stages of reaction, this one has exceptions to the rule. One of them was withdrawal: if an Aboriginal group had been badly mauled or wanted to avoid contact, they might physically withdraw from contact for a time. For example, some of the Bandjalang clans on the New South Wales north coast and the Walbiri of the central desert did this at different times.

By and large, however, accommodation or adaptation was inevitable for a conquered people. Most of the adjustments the Aborigines decided to make were concerned with material things and the economic side of life, and did not necessarily involve beliefs, values and culture. Hence, they freely accepted employment, but on their own terms. If a particular job no longer fulfilled a need, then the Aboriginal would simply abandon it, although certain Aborigines sometimes kept jobs for sentimental reasons — for instance, if they liked the boss.

In this context, it is worth remembering the vital assistance sometimes given to the famous explorers by Aborigines. Aborigines,

Accompanied by Edward J. Eyre, Wylie is welcomed back in Albany, WA, by his people after the two men traversed the Great Australian Bight from east to west in 1841.

never possessive, willingly shared waterholes and food with desperate or lost white men. What was considered heroism in European explorers was just everyday experience for Aborigines. Moreover, the courage and faithfulness of men like Wylie and Jackey Jackey deserve remembrance. It was not Edward Eyre alone who crossed the Great Australian Bight, for Wylie was with him. It was not E.B.C. Kennedy alone who braved the wilds of north Queensland; Jackey Jackey was there, stood by him when attacked by the local Aborigines, tended him when dying, buried his body and carried the story back. Indeed, thousands of Aboriginal people deserve to be remembered as pioneers in their own right, as shepherds, stockmen, trackers, housekeepers and nurses.

Aboriginal horse-breakers, stockmen and police trackers have been features of the frontier since the early years of settlement. During the gold rushes of the 1850s in particular, Aborigines accepted work as shepherds in control of large flocks, and also did other and varied work on sheep stations.

In this phase of accommodation, Aborigines in a sense merely adapted traditional hunting techniques, to obtain maximum return for minimum effort. Indeed, for many, begging and stealing became other forms of hunting and gathering with their own standard tactics of decoys and so on. In early Tasmania, hunting was improved enormously by the use of dogs taken or traded from Europeans. (There were no dingoes in Tasmania.)

Cultural Change

Confusion was increased for Aboriginal people by the fact that their traditional ways of explaining things to themselves could not cope with what was now happening. The loss of land often meant the loss, or weakening, of the spiritual ties which were so important. Sacred sites could be destroyed or fenced in. Those in a clan whose welfare was associated with the welfare of a particular animal might all have died, and this was thought to mean also the extinction of that animal. The boundaries of clans became confused, rules of social behaviour became useless or were broken more often, and tin cans replaced bangalow leaves as water containers. European ideas, mixed-blood children and the large number of deaths made marriage lines chaotic for generations.

The extent of these changes varied greatly. In central and northern Australia they have not yet gone all the way. Even in southern and eastern Australia, in some pockets, they had not gone very far by 1900. In more closely settled areas, however, the point of no return was probably reached between 1850 and 1880. In that period, most Aborigines in settled areas accepted residence on a station or mission as a compromise whereby their group life could be maintained and they could protect themselves against many of the consequences of being in white society. Not all of those consequences were negative: one strange consequence was that the status of women improved, for partly legal reasons. One of the last parts of ritual life to disappear was the initiation of young men: the last of these secret ceremonies held in New South Wales is believed to have been conducted in 1935. In much of northern Australia, they continued to be held.

In the early nineteenth century, Aborigines were notably reluctant to accept Christianity. Before the 1860s, there were not

Nalbert, a stockman at Oenpelli in the Northern Territory, 1950. Aboriginal stockmen were the backbone of the northern cattle industry for many years. (Photo by W. Brindle)

many acknowledged converts. Aboriginal people were willing to use the sanctuary afforded by missions and take gifts from the missionaries; in return, they allowed the missionaries to teach their children. In some cases, missionaries used the local languages but in others this was not practical. When traditional values such as reciprocity were strained or when marriage or burial customs were challenged, Aborigines could react strongly against the missionaries.

From the latter part of the nineteenth century, however, Aborigines in the settled areas were showing increasing interest in Christianity. For many on the reserves and missions, the church or chapel had become an important part of communal life. Literacy and the values of justice and equality taught by Christian missionaries were occasionally used by converts to write petitions and letters of protest to authorities. Some Aboriginal Christians testified that Christianity filled the spiritual void left by the collapse of traditional values and culture. Alternatively, Christianity was seen by tribal Aborigines as an extension of traditional beliefs, and they could incorporate the best of old beliefs, practices, values, worship forms and art in their new faith. (Bark paintings in lieu of stained-glass windows are a striking example.)

On the other hand, however, others have thumbed their noses at European values and beliefs, at least partly because of Europeans' hypocrisy in not sticking to their own standards of fair play when dealing with Aborigines. Sometimes Aborigines have poured scorn

The Rev. Lazarus Lamilami pictured in his church on Croker Island, NT, in 1971. He was the first Aboriginal Methodist minister. Here we see the Christian message expressed in Aboriginal artwork.

on the new-fangled white religion; sometimes they have flaunted different standards of behaviour and, deliberately or not, given offence to white communities.   Continued adherence to the 'old way' was certainly a form of resistance — cultural instead of military.

Music, dance and sport of the European kinds became increasingly   popular   in Aboriginal   communities. They were adapted and shaped by Aboriginal culture and experience. Gospel and country music and gum-leaf bands, local dances and football, running and boxing became widely popular in settled   districts. Accommodation

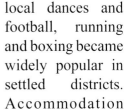

Troopers John Ling-woodock and James Geary pictured with their new brides in Brisbane in 1917 before going to the Middle East with the Australian Light Horse. Jim Geary was very seriously wounded. Stockmen's skills were in demand in the Light Horse.

or adaptation was definitely a case of an Aboriginal 'self-help' (or a 'help yourself') policy.

In the Great War of 1914–18, despite its being illegal for Aborigines to join the Army, over 300 did so. Many were from country areas and used their skills in the Light Horse. Some were killed, injured or taken prisoner, but their service and sacrifices, as Indigenous people, were not acknowledged.

READING 5

Aboriginal Adaptation in the Nineteenth Century

That Aborigines could take advantage of the adverse conditions arising from white settlement is indicated in the following extracts from reports to the Board for the Protection of the Aborigines of New South Wales for 1896.

The four reserves in the Gladstone district are now all securely fenced, cleared, and under cultivation. The aborigines now reap good crops, and are in a fair way of living.

At Nymboida, good three-roomed dwellings have been erected. A portion of the land has been fenced, cleared, and placed under cultivation; the remainder has been ringbarked with a view to putting a larger area under crop next season.

The aborigines at Walcha Road placed 20 acres under wheat, oats, and potatoes last season. They have also greatly improved their reserve by fencing, ringbarking, etc.

One of the reserves in the Kempsey district has been enclosed with a good two-railed fence, and sub-divided into three paddocks. Twelve acres are under maize.

One the reserve at Sherwood, about 25 acres have been cleared of scrub and heavy timber. The aborigines are about to enclose the land with a substantial fence.

On the reserve at Euroka Creek good progress continues to be made. One aboriginal has, in addition to a comfortable dwelling, erected a good straddle barn with bark roof. He keeps a lot of poultry, has 9 acres under maize, potatoes, and vegetables, and has enclosed 25 acres with a good dogleg and superior pole fence. Another has erected a log pig-style, stockyard, and calf-pen, has a number of fruit-trees growing, and 8 acres fenced and under maize and potatoes. Another has erected a skillion slab hut with bark roof, and has 7 acres fenced and under maize.

The aborigines at Currowan grow maize and potatoes on their reserve, and keep a cow and fowls.

The reserve at Minnamurra was only set apart towards the end of the year. The aborigines have already erected three dwellings, have cleared and burnt off a portion of the land, and have dug up and planted garden plots.

The aborigines at Bushfield have erected dwellings for themselves, have fenced in a vegetable garden, and intend cultivating other portions of the land.

New South Wales Parliament, *Votes and Proceedings*, 1897, Vol. VII, p. 884.

QUESTIONS FOR READING 5

How much paternalism (on the part of white people) and how much self-help (on the part of black people) was involved in the sort of policies described in Reading 5?

What view of 'progress' is held by the writers of the reports?

FURTHER READING

Jackomos, A., and D. Fowell, *Forgotten Heroes — Aborigines at War From the Somme to Vietnam,* Melbourne: Victoria Press, 1993.

McGrath, A., *'Born in the Cattle': Aborigines in Cattle Country*, Sydney: Allen & Unwin, 1987.

Reynolds, H., *Black Pioneers*, Melbourne: Penguin, 2000.

6   Poverty and Protest

Poverty does not simply mean lack of money. Poverty has social, cultural and spiritual aspects as well as material, and in a society as closely woven together as that of the Aboriginal, a breakdown in one aspect led almost inevitably to breakdown in another. For too many Aboriginal people, at least before the 1960s, 'demoralization' describes their situation as well as 'poverty'. The new generation always seemed to show less interest in their heritage than in the white men's gadgets, be they tomahawks or taxis.

Population Decline

The drastic decline of the Aboriginal population was one of the biggest factors in their impoverishment and certainly the most obvious. By the 1840s the original inhabitants of Sydney and Melbourne had disappeared, leaving a handful of 'mixed bloods' who belonged to neither society. By the 1870s, the 'full-blood' Tasmanians had disappeared. Why this decrease from over 500,000 in 1788 to about 60,000 in 1921? An unknown number of part-Aborigines in 1921 did not wish to be counted as Aborigines, but this makes no difference to the basic fact: catastrophic population decline (see the table on p. 69).

William Westgarth, an acute observer of early Victoria, suggested in 1846 four main causes of Aboriginal depopulation. Firstly, he suggested, was war among themselves and hostilities with whites. The former was

not very significant; though it is understandable that a clan displaced
form its own territory by whites could infringe another clan's country
and cause hostility. War with the whites was a far bigger cause. To
generalize, in areas where the decline was greatest — Tasmania, parts
of Queensland and Western Australia — this was possibly the biggest
factor. Variety was great: for instance, in the Northern Rivers region
of New South Wales, this first cause was of quite minor importance. It
is impossible to be very definite about other areas, but the second and
third causes were generally ahead of this one.

'Getting Near.' This cartoon reflected the belief of the time that
the Aboriginal population was doomed. (Glover, *The Bulletin*,
1927)

Secondly, Westgarth stressed the importance of disease in depopulation, especially venereal disease. Aborigines were very vulnerable to European-introduced diseases against which they had no resistance, especially smallpox, measles, dysentery and influenza. These were the biggest killers. It is believed that many thousands died in three great smallpox epidemics of 1789, 1829–31 and the 1860s. There has been much debate about the origins of the first of these, with suggestions of deliberate 'germ warfare'. There was no evidence of smallpox on the First Fleet and a northern origin (the Macassans) of the first epidemic has been suggested.

ABORIGINAL AND TORRES STRAIT ISLANDER POPULATION, 1788–2006

State or Territory	1788[1]	1788[2]	1921[3]	1966[4]	1971[5]	1996[6]	2006[7]
NSW	40,000	152,000	6,067	13,613	23,109	93,996	138,507
ACT	–	–	0	96	248	2,712	3,872
Vic.	11,500	42,000	573	1,790	5,656	18,384	30,143
Qld	100,000	285,000	15,454	19,003	24,414	74,394	127,580
SA	10,000	30,000	2,741	5,505	7,140	18,942	25,557
WA	52,000	142,000	17,671	18,439	21,903	48,996	58,711
Tas.	4,000	5,000	0	55	573	12,023	16,767
NT	35,000	95,000	17,973	21,119	23,253	44,486	53,662
TOTAL	252,500	750,000	60,479	79,620	106,288	314,120	455,025

[1] A. R. Radcliffe-Brown's estimate in the *Official Year Book of the Commonwealth of Australia*, XXIII, 1930, pp. 672, 687–96, updated for Tasmania. The total is a minimum figure and Radcliffe-Brown's figure is usually given as 300,000. There were probably about 5000 Torres Strait Islanders.

[2] These figures are based on the estimates of N.G. Butlin, *Our Original Aggression*, and those of other more recent scholars and represent the best estimate possible at this stage.

[3] *Official Year Book of the Commonwealth of Australia*, XVII, 1924, pp. 951–61. (To the ACT figure, the population of Wreck Bay should be added.)

[4] *1966 Census*: Statement on the Aboriginal Population.

[5] *The Australian Aboriginals*, Australian Information Service Publication, 1974, p. 3.

[6] 1996 *Census*. (These figures *exclude* Torres Strait Islanders; there were 28,744 of them). Note the remarkable increase, especially in Tasmania.

[7] 2006 *Census*. (These figures *include* 29,512 Torres Strait Islanders and 17,811 of mixed TSI and Aboriginal descent; of these, approximately 6800 were living in the Torres Strait region.)

Note on 1971 and 1996/2006 Figures

The exponential increase in population after 1966 can be explained by various factors. First, the referendum of 1967 officially approved the counting of Aborigines in the census for the first time. Secondly, there was a consequent rapidly growing pride in Aboriginality, which accounts for the rise to a greater extent than the third factor, actual population growth, especially in New South Wales and Tasmania — though that was considerable. Furthermore, by the 1990s the majority of Indigenous people in marriage and similar relationships were in partnerships with non-Indigenous people: in 2001 this was 69 per cent. Contrary to earlier tendencies, their children are very likely to identify as indigenous, thus multiplying the population figures even more. For reasons which are somewhat mysterious, these growth factors are even more potent in Tasmania, although it should be noted that there have been allegations within the Aboriginal community of illegitimate claims to Aboriginal ancestry there (related to entitlement to vote in ATSIC elections or to receive benefits). The 2006 Census total of 455,031 represented an increase of 11 per cent over the 2001 figure. The biggest proportional increases were in the Northern Territory and New South Wales. By 2007, the Indigenous population reached half a million, of whom 100,000 lived in Sydney, Brisbane and Perth.

Alcoholism merely added to the general health problem: for instance, in colder areas alcohol and exposure led to respiratory diseases and pneumonia. Venereal disease was extremely common: some nineteenth-century observers though half the adult Aborigines had a form of it. Though few deaths were directly caused by venereal disease, it induced sterility and reduced the birth-rate, which was very low until well into the last century. Children were worst affected by disease, and the infant mortality rate of Aborigines has always been high partly as a result.

Infant mortality was Westgarth's third point. Living with disease in depressing conditions must also have contributed to a lower birth-rate, with parents less willing to have children. Malnutrition became more damaging as time went on; this is related to the next point. Diseases like anaemia, gastroenteritis and pneumonia were common diseases of poor people and therefore also common amongst Aboriginal people.

Fourthly, there were the conditions in which Aborigines lived, and their means of support. In pastoral areas, Aboriginal food supplies (animals and birds, for example) were seriously endangered and the white man's rations were often lacking in protein. In colder areas, blankets and clothes were often a poor substitute for possum-skin rugs. The combined effect of causes two, three and four was to keep Aborigines in a vicious circle of disease, poverty and death.

An important aspect of poverty was a loss of pride and confidence resulting from the loss of traditional skills, territory and way of life. The death of so many people and the increasing number of children 'without fathers' (so-called 'half-castes') caused severe social problems. Though many Aborigines were employed, their wages were usually much lower than those of white workers. This was bad enough, but in the white economy the previously highly valued Aboriginal skills and tools were now valued in terms of money and by that measure many of them were close to valueless. The replacement of stone tools by more efficient steel tools also caused changes in work and social patterns within communities.

Variations From Pauperism
There were variations from the pattern of pauperization. One of the

most interesting was 'nativism', that is, a going back to traditional beliefs, withdrawing mentally (and even physically) to build a new-old pattern of life and defy the white world. On the United States frontier at the end of the nineteenth century, the ghost dance swept through and stirred up Native American groups; similarly some Aborigines in the twentieth century attempted to reassert old values in a new situation. A classic example is the religious movement in the 1940s and 1950s among Bandjalang clans of northern New South Wales. Aboriginal mythology, ceremonies and belief were intermixed with Pentecostal Christianity to form a unique blend and renew group solidarity and confidence. Allied with this was the increasing use of their own language, even in the presence of whites. In even more recent years, attempts have been made by some urban Aborigines to introduce their 'detribalized' fellows to aspects of traditional culture, with the aim of renewing self-respect.

A contradictory variation is the phenomenon of 'passing', whereby light-skinned Aborigines faded into white society and over generations 'forgot' their Aborig-inality. No one knows the exact extent of this, but it was fairly common between 1850 and 1950.

Towards the end of the nineteenth century on some of the reserves and

Pictured in 1876, two ladies and two children of Coranderrk, Victoria, display confidence and respectability in the face of discrimination.

stations, notably Coranderrk in Victoria, Raukkan in South Australia and Cumeroogunga in New South Wales, the Aboriginal resi-dents had developed into self-supporting and proudly independent communities. Though governments could have encouraged these developments, Raukkan was broken up in 1894, and Coranderrk broke up between 1886 and 1923, both as a direct result of government discouragement. Cumeroogunga's enterprise faded out in the 1920s also. This was despite petitions and protests by residents and the efforts of some white supporters. These developments were a kind of 'second dispossession'.

Better known are those individual Aborigines who broke the race barrier and escaped impoverishment by heroic self-effort, great proficiency in a particular field and sympathetic assistance from white people. There have been three main fields where this has happened. Firstly, the church enabled Aborigines to take leadership roles, including Pastor Frank Roberts in New South Wales, Pastor Sir Douglas Nicholls in Victoria, Deacon James and Angelina Noble in Queensland and Western Australia, and James

David Unaipon, lay preacher, author and inventor, a Ngarrindjerri man from Point Macleay, SA, as pictured on the $50 note.

Sir Douglas Nicholls, champion athlete and footballer, pastor and later (in 1976, pictured here) Governor of South Australia.

An Aboriginal cricket team in Victoria in 1866, the core of the team which toured England in 1868.

and David Unaipon in South Australia.

Secondly, many Aborigines became prominent in sport. In 1868 the first Australian cricket team to tour England was composed entirely of Aborigines, who played 47 matches, including many against county teams, and won fourteen of them. Mullagh, Lawrence and Cuzens performed brilliantly with both bat and ball. In the 1930s Eddie Gilbert was a tearaway fast bowler for Queensland, alleged to be able to bowl at 180km/h, and who clean bowled Don Bradman. It has been estimated that 15 per cent of Australian boxing champions have been Aboriginal. In the 1940s, Dave Sands and Ron Richards were world-class fighters and Geoff Dynevor won Olympic and Commonwealth Games medals in 1960 and 1962.

In the arts, too, individual Aborigines broke the barriers. In the 1950s, Robert Tudawali and Ngarla Kunoth had transient fame through the film *Jedda*. The Aranda camel-boy Albert Namatjira grasped the opportunity to learn to paint in watercolours from Rex Battarbee

The climactic scene from the film *Jedda* (1955), in which the characters Marbuck (Robert Tudawali) and Jedda (Ngarla Kunoth) are about to go over the cliff.

and became famous. Harold Blair was a popular tenor in the 1950s and 1960s. Jimmy Little had a number one hit in 1963 with a gospel song, 'Royal Telephone'. Kath Walker (later Oodgeroo Noonuccal) published her first book of verse, *We Are Going*, in 1964, and a year later Colin Johnson (later Mudrooroo) published his first novel, *Wild Cat Falling*.

Two important reservations need to be made about all this. Firstly, the individual exceptions were few and isolated until the 1970s, although they have become more numerous since then. Secondly, the white society has applauded success in particular fields, but has often frustrated the successful by its general repressiveness: the Aboriginal champion might have been accepted as a sporting freak, but not as a person. Rejection by a two-faced white society, sometimes accompanied by a retreat to the friendship of alcohol resulting in oblivion or death, was the fate of a number of these heroes. Thus, success was a dead end for Namatjira; as Martin Luther King, Jr said, while one is not free none is completely free.

Harold Blair from Purga mission near Ipswich, Queensland, found fame as a tenor in the 1950s.

Poet Kath Walker later took the name Oodgeroo Noonuccal and worked for the cultural revival of her Noonuccal people of Stradbroke Island, south-east Queensland.

The Dimensions of Poverty

Despite all the advances in recent years, these and other individual successes over the years, and great diversity in the Aboriginal community, the fact remains that after 180 years the Aborigines were by far the most disadvantaged group in Australia. This fact can be traced in all areas of life. In the late 1960s, a survey of Aboriginal housing in New South Wales revealed that of the 'houses', 37 per cent were shacks, 51 per cent had not enough beds, 38 per cent had no water supply and 41 per cent had no garbage disposal. It is no wonder that gastric and respiratory diseases exacted such a heavy toll of Aboriginal lives, especially young ones.

Probably the gravest problem was that even with a growing population because of a high birth-rate, the infant mortality rate of Aborigines was more than six times the national average. In fact, in 1972, 40 per cent of Aboriginal deaths occurred in the first year of life compared with the total Australian figure of 4 per cent. Malnutrition, especially the lack of vitamin C, handicapped the survivors not only physically but mentally. Eye diseases, especially in rural areas, were another major problem, as is leprosy: in the Kimberleys in 1970 perhaps 10 per cent of the Aboriginal population had this disease. Venereal disease, tuberculosis and very prevalent alcoholism made the situation even more depressing.

In the field of education, an Aboriginal child in 1971 had one thirtieth the chance of a white child of finishing high school. Between 1964 and 1971 the educational gap between white and black actually widened. Before 1973, a mere handful had reached university and no 'full-blood' Aboriginal had even matriculated. At every level, Aborigines derived far less benefit from education, which is after all planned for pupils with a 'normal' (that is, white Australian) background.

Education was not and is not a solution by itself. This point is illustrated by the 1966 statistic that 63 of the 103 Aborigines who had matriculated were manual labourers. In fact, about 70 per cent of working Aborigines in 1971 were manual labourers, compared with about 30 per cent of working Australians as a whole. The unemployment rate was three to four times that of the general community, and even then, a high proportion was in jobs that were seasonal or provided irregular

A family from northern New South Wales camped on the outskirts of Brisbane in 1890. Though the housing was poor, they were well-dressed.

employment. Not until 1968 did Aborigines in the cattle industry in the Northern Territory receive wages equal to those of whites. With few exceptions, Aborigines were consistently and badly underpaid all over the continent for at least 180 years. It is no wonder that Aborigines in the past tended to show little loyalty to jobs.

Health, education, employment and housing formed a vicious circle for Aborigines, a circle made more vicious in too many cases by the intrusion of legal discrimination. This operated in three ways: firstly, laws for the protection of all are sometimes ignored or not enforced for Aborigines; secondly, special laws in many instances took from Aborigines the rights of other citizens; and thirdly, some laws even when justly operated were unjust in practice because of Aborigines' different needs. As a result, about twenty times too many prisoners, proportional to population, were Aboriginal.

As much through the efforts of Aboriginal groups and individuals as anything else, the 'vicious circle' effect has been lessened, even if far from removed. Since the early 1970s, many aspects of Aboriginal health and education have shown steady, if slow, improvement. This story belongs in the next chapter.

Protest and Political Action by Aborigines
In order to break out of the vicious circle, political organization was necessary. Until the 1930s, protest and political action by Aborigines had been local and isolated and easily ignored or crushed by protection boards and politicians. In the 1920s and 1930s, some outstanding individuals emerged to coordinate protests and unite the divided and scattered demands for 'citizen rights'. In 1925 Fred Maynard and other men from the near north coast of New South Wales launched the Australian Aboriginal Progressive Association. The AAPA protested against the loss of reserves and demanded that children should not be taken from their families, that Aboriginal families should receive land grants, that Aboriginal children should be free to attend public schools and that Aborigines should control any administrative body which affected them.

In the mid-1930s, William Cooper in Victoria collected hundreds of signatures on a petition to the King. With Doug Nicholls and Margaret Tucker, he began the Australian Aborigines' League. The petition, asking for equal political rights, never reached the King because it was 'killed' by the federal government. In New South Wales, the founders of the Aborigines' Progressive Association, William Ferguson and Jack Patten, organized a 'day of mourning and protest' for Australia Day in 1938 which was attended by delegates from New South Wales and Victoria. Shortly after, the APA set up a newspaper called *Abo Call*, which lasted six months.

William Cooper, the Yorta Yorta man from Victoria who attempted to petition the King in the 1930s. He wanted seats in federal parliament for Aboriginal people. One of his sons had been killed fighting for his country in the war of 1914–18.

The following year, 1939, saw the famous strike at the Murray River Aboriginal station, Cumeroogunga. In the 1920s, large sections of the reserve had been leased to white farmers. By 1939, the housing conditions were squalid, health and rations poor and the manager tyrannical. The people unsuccessfully petitioned the New South Wales Aborigines' Protection Board to replace the manager. Jack Patten urged the Cumeroogunga people to take action and was arrested while addressing the residents. Many residents then left Cumeroogunga and crossed the Murray into Victoria. The strike failed because conditions across the Murray were even worse and the Victorian government stopped dole payments to the strikers and prevented their children from attending school. Nevertheless, the strike was important because it

A group outside the Australian Hall in Sydney on 26 January 1938. Bill Ferguson is on the left and Jack Patten on the right.

gained publicity about conditions on reserves and stations, for the just demands of the Aboriginal people and provided encouragement for the movement for Aboriginal rights generally. In 1940 the New South Wales Aborigines' Protection Board was replaced by the Aborigines' Welfare Board and was given more funding, especially for housing. Not long after, Aboriginal people were given the right to elect two representatives onto the board. William Ferguson was one of these and later still he stood unsuccessfully for election to federal parliament.

The Second World War was important for all Australians. Despite their 'second-class' status, about 3000 Aborigines joined up to defend their country. In the armed forces and as civilians employed by the army, Aborigines were treated completely equally, itself a wonderful experience. Perhaps they were hoping that they would be now more widely recognized as equal citizens. But this was not to be for, after the war, Aboriginal veterans found that they were expected to fall back into the old pattern of discrimination. This experience moved many of these men and women to use skills learned in the forces to become

Reg Saunders served in the Australian Army 1940–45 and 1951–54 and became the first Aboriginal army officer in 1944. Later he was a welfare worker and public servant.

active in fighting for the rights of their people.

Just after the war, in 1949, an Australia-wide umbrella organization was set up, the Federal Council for Aboriginal Advancement (which later became the Federal Council for the Advancement of Aborigines and Torres Strait Islanders, or FCAATSI for short). In 1961, the One People of Australia League (OPAL) was established in Queensland for Aboriginal advancement.

The strike is a common self-help workers' protest but it had not been tried by Aboriginal workers before the war. In 1946, cattle industry workers of the Pilbara area of Western Australia went on strike over pay and conditions and supported themselves for over 30 years by fossicking for tin and some rare minerals. They came to be known as the Nomads. Though assisted by a white man, Don McLeod, their efforts at community development were an example of self-effort on a heroic scale in very adverse conditions. Otherwise, however, it was not until the 1960s that many non-urban Aborigines began to realize the possibilities of their acting politically themselves.

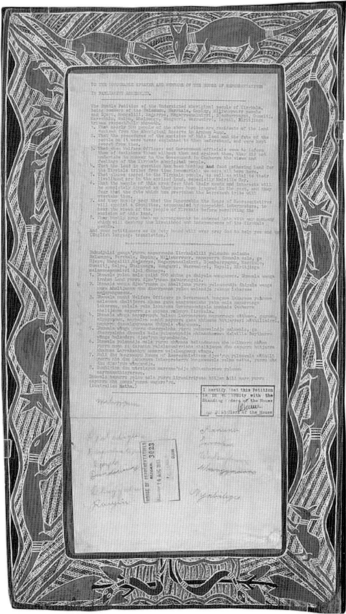

The famous 'Bark Petition' of 1963, in the Gamatj language and English, sent by Yolngu people of Yirrkala, NT, to the federal parliament. It was a protest at their loss of land to a mining company.

READING 6

Aboriginal Political Agitation in the 1930s

The mid-1930s saw Aborigines organizing themselves on a wider basis to demand their rights, using the traditional means of petition, public meetings and publications. The authors of this extract organized the Day of Mourning on Australia Day 1938.

ONE HUNDRED AND FIFTY YEARS

The 26th of January, 1938, is not a day of rejoicing for Australia's Aborigines; it is a day of mourning. This festival of 150 years' so-called 'progress' in Australia commemorates also 150 years of misery and degradation imposed upon the original native inhabitants by the white invaders of this country. We, representing the Aborigines now ask you, the reader of this appeal, to pause in the midst of your sesqui-centenary rejoicings and ask yourself honestly whether your 'conscience' is clear in regard to the treatment of the Australian blacks by the Australian whites during the period of 150 years' history which you celebrate?

THE OLD AUSTRALIANS

You are the New Australians, but we are the Old Australians. We have in our arteries the blood of the Original Australians, who have lived in this land for many thousands of years. You came here only recently, and you took our land away from us by force. You have almost exterminated our people, but there are enough of us remaining to expose the humbug of your claim, as white Australians, to be a civilized, progressive, kindly and humane nation. By your cruelty and callousness towards the Aborigines you stand condemned in the eyes of the civilized world.

PLAIN SPEAKING

These are hard words, but we ask you to face the truth of our accusation. If you would openly admit that the purpose of your Aborigines Legislation has been, and now is, to exterminate the Aborigines completely so that not a trace of them or of their descendants remains, we could describe you as brutal, but honest. But you dare not admit openly that your hope and wish is for our death! You hypocritically claim that you are trying to 'protect' us; but your modern policy of 'protection' (so-called) is killing us off just as surely as the pioneer policy of giving us poisoned damper and shooting us down like dingoes!

We ask you now, reader, to put your mind, as a citizen of the Australian Commonwealth, to the facts presented in these pages. We ask you to study the problem, in the way that we present the case, from the Aborigines' point of view. We do not ask for your charity; we do not ask you to study us as scientific freaks. Above all, we do not ask for your 'protection', No, thanks! We have had 150 years of that! We ask only for justice, decency and fair play. Is this too much to ask? Surely your minds and hearts are not so callous that you will refuse to reconsider your policy of degrading and humiliating and exterminating Old Australia's Aborigines?

William Ferguson and Jack Patten, *Aborigines Claim Citizen Rights*,
Sydney, 1938.

QUESTIONS FOR READING 6

Why do the authors reject 'protection' policies?

What is the basis for their claim for 'citizen rights'?

FURTHER READING

Attwood, B., and A. Markus, *The Struggle for Aboriginal Rights: A Documentary History*, Sydney: Allen & Unwin, 1999.

Haebich, A., *Broken Circles: Fragmenting Indigenous Families, 1800–2000*, Fremantle: Fremantle Arts Centre Press, 2000.

Maynard, J., *Flight for Liberty and Freedom: The Origins of Australian Aboriginal Activism*, Canberra: Aboriginal Studies Press, 2007.

7 Since 1967

Until the 1960s, 'assimilation' was supposed to be the ultimate goal for Aborigines, but this was a goal decided upon in the late 1930s by white governments, not by Aboriginal people themselves. Except for part-Aborigines who passed as whites, and individual success stories, assimilation was not a realistic goal, anyway. To be assimilated into white society, one had to be accepted as an equal by that society. And so assimilation also offended Aborigines by implying the inferiority of Aboriginal culture. The modified policy of 1965 — integration — was also rejected by Aboriginal leaders, who advocated self-determination. This advocacy, coordinated by the Federal Council for the Advancement of Aborigines and Torres Strait Islanders, led to the success of the 1967 referendum (see Chapter 11 below). Aboriginal leaders also helped influence governments after 1967 to adopt more constructive policies which attempted to assist the development of action for Aborigines by Aborigines. Finally, most governments actually accepted the aim of self-determination in the 1970s themselves.

Changing Directions

For a variety of reasons, there was a great upsurge in action in Aboriginal affairs from about 1965, especially by Aborigines. Some of the reasons have little to do with Aborigines themselves. The fact that they had been steadily moving into the capital cities since the Second World

War has meant that many more white Australians than ever before became personally aware of Aborigines, and enabled Aborigines of different regional backgrounds to meet and to share their concerns. Those Indigenous Australians who had served in the Second World War, briefly experienced equality but then returned to their former position after the war, were now able to apply their leadership skills in the Aboriginal rights movement.

Instead of merely responding to the alternatives proposed by white well-wishers, Aborigines were doing more of their own protesting and community work; most importantly, they were increasingly setting their own goals. In this they were assisted by some governments and churches, which enabled the residents of reserve and mission lands to incorporate and to own as a body the land on which they lived. Aboriginal communities responded by seeking to develop new industries, sometimes employing white experts to help them in their aims.

A cartoon comment on half-hearted reform after the 1967 referendum.

Growing in confidence through older organizations such as FCAATSI, Aborigines branched out in a number of directions, political and otherwise. It was symptomatic that in 1970 the all-black National Tribal Council split away from FCAATSI over the issue of whether the Federal Council should have any white people involved in running it. In the 1970s, black power advocates like Bruce McGuinness in Victoria and Denis Walker in Queensland gained more prominence as Aboriginal spokesmen. There was disappointment that the referendum success did not lead to rapid progress on land rights and other issues. This was part of the reason for the Aboriginal Tent Embassy set up on the lawns of federal Parliament House in Canberra in 1972. It made a dramatic impact. Paul Coe unsuccessfully sued the Commonwealth

The Aboriginal Tent Embassy, Canberra, 1972.

Michael Mansell, Tasmanian lawyer, militant campaigner and leader of the Provisional Aboriginal Government.

of Australia in 1979, asserting Aboriginal sovereignty and seeking enormous damages. A Provisional Aboriginal Government was declared by radicals, including Michael Mansell of Tasmania. The next generation of leaders in the 1980s, like Gary Foley and Pat Dodson, were skilled politicians who had learned from the experiences of the previous two decades.

Cooperative action for Aboriginal community development became more common. The Aboriginal residents of Cabbage Tree Island, on the Richmond River in northern New South Wales, formed the Numbahging Co-Operative in 1960 to farm sugar cane and improve their economic position generally. The Gurindji of the Northern Territory became famous in 1966 when they went on strike; they soon requested that some of their own land be returned to them. Finally, in August 1975, their land was given back by the Commonwealth government. In the early 1970s, in inner-city areas like Redfern and Fitzroy, Aborigines organised medical and legal services, which deal with two of the most serious problems facing Aborigines: ill-health and discrimination. Aboriginal alcoholism projects were also begun in Redfern, Moree, Brisbane and elsewhere.

From the early 1970s, the participation of Aborigines in all levels of education increased. By the early 1980s, over 7000 Aborigines were enrolled in further or higher education. By the late 1980s, hundreds had graduated from universities and colleges, including some with higher degrees. Eric Willmot became director of the Australian Institute of Aboriginal Studies and then the first Aboriginal professor. At the then South Australian College of Advanced Education, Macquarie University and elsewhere, Aborigines began to teach Aboriginal studies. Aboriginal teachers and aides were recruited and trained in order to bridge the gap between schools and Aboriginal communities. Independent Aboriginal schools have been established, such as Worowa College, Frankston, the Black Community School in Townsville and Yiparinya in Alice Springs. Aboriginal Education Consultative Groups were established at state and federal level to give a boost to Aboriginal studies and advice to education departments.

Aborigines of various shades of political opinion began to seize political opportunities in the 1970s. The National Aboriginal Consultative Committee, first elected in 1974, encouraged the formation of political demands by Aborigines themselves. It was split up and reorganized as the National Aboriginal Conference and the Council for Aboriginal Development in 1977. Ironically, perhaps, the first Aboriginal parliamentarian was the fairly conservative Senator Neville Bonner, a Queensland Liberal who was regarded by younger radicals as an 'Uncle Tom' or a 'Jacky'. Moderate

Neville Bonner, pictured in 1979, was the first Aboriginal member of parliament. He was a Liberal Senator for Queensland from 1971 to 1983.

Aboriginal leaders, such as Pastor Sir Douglas Nicholls and Senator Bonner and their white supporters believed more could be done by cooperation, and feared a white backlash against Aborigines if black power went too far or if governments gave too much too soon. Senator Bonner suggested that those seeking to reassert Aboriginal values ought to accept one of them themselves: namely, that deference and obedience should be paid to the elders. The more militant, such as Paul Coe, Denis Walker, Bobbi Sykes and Charles Perkins, replied that caution played into the hands of white racists who wanted to delay justice for as long as possible. It was said by the black radicals that a revolution may be necessary. Revolutions seem to occur not so much

Charles Perkins, who led the
Freedom Ride in 1965, is pictured
here as a public servant in 1974.
He later became head of the federal
Department of Aboriginal Affairs,
1984–89.

when conditions get worse but rather when they are improving, but too slowly. This was certainly the case in Aboriginal affairs in Australia in the early 1970s. Revolution did not look likely; but violence was a strong possibility.

With the limited granting of land rights from 1977, local land councils began to give new opportunities for Aboriginal self-management, and threw up new leaders such as Galarrwuy Yunupingu of the Northern Territory. Aborigines began to run cattle stations, such as Willowra (NT), Delta Downs (Qld) and Kenmore Park (SA). The 'out-station movement' also developed, whereby many Aboriginal people chose to go back to their traditional way of life. By the late 1980s, there were over 160 such communities with nearly 4000 members, mostly in central and northern Australia. Founded in 1981, the Aboriginal Development Commission provided for self-management on a broad scale, acquiring land and financing commercial ventures and housing. One unusual enterprise in the far north was Applied Ecology Pty Ltd, which farmed crocodiles in Queensland and emus in Western Australia in the 1970s.

Despite the impressive improvements in the 1970s and 1980s, the gap between the standards of living of the black and white communities remained wide. Aborigines still had a much lower life expectancy and educational attainment and higher rates of disease (including leprosy, trachoma and venereal diseases), unemployment and imprisonment.

In the 1970s and 1980s, diversity in culture was increasing and Australians were gradually embracing the new approach of multiculturalism, becoming more tolerant of differences. Greater stress on Aboriginality encouraged this and, in turn, was encouraged by it. The rate of marriage between Aboriginal and non-Aboriginal partners was high and increasing but absorption of this kind did not mean that Aborigines adopted, willy-nilly, the 'white' way of life. Aborigines were not giving up their traditions and, at the same time, white Australians were much more accepting and appreciative of Aboriginal culture. Mingling of cultures increased rather than merely the continued absorption of one by the other. Maintenance of culture was a major aim of Aboriginal organization from the 1970s and 1980s.

In the 1970s, some Aboriginal leaders talked of 'black nationalism', some of 'pan-Aboriginalism'; others predicted that blood would be shed in the cause of Aboriginal freedom. Though white people were alarmed by the use of the term 'black power', it did not necessarily imply violence. Radicals, and not only radicals, were asserting that 'blacks' should have power over their own lives; that they should not be controlled by state governments, adverse social circumstances or the interests of mining companies or the cattle industry. Some went further in the 1970s and said that this freedom should be won by force. They tended to be an urban minority and this did not come about, but increased conflict, agitation and friction did. By the 1980s, however, strategies became more realistic, though tougher, involving working through government and the law courts. The remarkable reawakening within the Aboriginal communities of Australia in the 1960s and 1970s gave the Aborigines more influence as a group and as a public issue than they had known since 1850.

Aboriginal Achievement Since the 1970s
Entrepreneurship has become gradually increasingly important through cooperatives, the management and reinvestment of mining royalty payments and other initiatives. In 1983, John Kundereri Moriarty established the Jumbana Group, now Australia's leading indigenous art and design company. He and his wife run Balarinji design studio in Sydney. In 1994 and 1995, they were commissioned to paint two

Qantas jumbo jets in Aboriginal designs. The Australian and Torres Strait Islander Commission (ATSIC) chairman appointed in 1996 was Gatjil Djerrkura, a successful businessman in the Northern Territory. However, most of the tiny Aboriginal middle class which started to emerge remained directly or indirectly dependent on government.

In 1986, Arthur Malcolm was consecrated the first Aboriginal bishop in the Anglican Church and in the 1990s, the Rev. Djiniyini Gondarra was elected Moderator of the Northern Synod of the Uniting Church. Nungalinyah College in Darwin and Wontulp College in Townsville were established to train leaders for the churches in an authentically Aboriginal theological context.

Sport continued to be a field in which Aborigines could excel and therefore gain acceptance in a sport-mad country. In tennis, there was Evonne Goolagong, top boxers such as Lionel Rose and Tony Mundine, and soccer players Charles Perkins (also the second Aboriginal university graduate) and Harry Williams, who played in the World Cup finals in 1974. In the early 1980s, the three Ella brothers made a big impact in rugby union, especially on the 1984 tour of the British Isles with the Wallabies. Arthur Beetson, Larry Corowa, Steve Renouf and Johnathan Thurston were but four of many who have played for Australia in rugby league. In Australian Rules, Maurice Rioli captained Richmond in the 1982 grand final while the Krakouer brothers starred for North Melbourne and in 1993 Gavin Wanganeen won the Brownlow Medal. In 1994, Cathy Freeman won two gold medals at the Auckland Commonwealth Games, where she flew the Aboriginal flag. In 2000 at the Sydney Olympics, she lit

Glen Ella, one of three brothers from Sydney to play for the rugby union Wallabies.

the Olympic torch and won the gold medal in the 400 metres.

A cultural and creative renaissance occurred from the 1960s and 1970s, in painting and other arts, dance, drama and film, poetry and novels. Dick Roughsey from Mornington Island became well known as a painter and storyteller in the 1970s. Painters and potters have grown in number, without compromising their Aboriginal styles. Painting has become a growth industry for several remote communities and 'traditional' art and design has taken on the world. A 'black theatre' emerged, with a company formed in Melbourne in 1972 by actor Bob Maza and others. Jack Davis was a notable poet (for example, *The First Born,* 1970) and

Cathy Freeman, the outstanding sprinter from Queensland.

playwright, starting with the strong historical drama *No Sugar* in 1985. In 1986 Sally Morgan's story of family and self-discovery, *My Place,* was published and became a bestseller. The Aboriginal Islander Dance Theatre began in 1976 and went on from strength to strength. The Bangarra Dance Theatre emerged after 1989 and has toured overseas extensively over the last decade.

In the renaissance of Australian film in the 1970s and 1980s, Aborigines have been prominent, including Tommy Lewis, Justine Saunders, David Gulpilil and Mawayul Yanthalawuy. In the 1990s, Rachel Perkins and Tracey Moffatt directed feature films. One of the top films of 2006 was *Ten Canoes*, starring the by-then-veteran actor David Gulpilil and his son Jamie. The Aboriginal TV service, Imparja, began transmission in Central Australia in 1987. Aboriginal performers have forced their way into the 'mainstream' of popular culture, such as Deborah Mailman, Ernie Dingo, Christine Anu and Troy Cassar-

Daly. *Bran Nue Dae*, a musical by Jimmy Chi, was first performed at the 1990 Perth Festival. In 1992, the Aboriginal rock group, Yothu Yindi, won five Australian Record Industry Association (ARIA) awards. Their song, 'Treaty', was a big hit. Torres Strait Islander Christine Anu's song, 'My Island Home', won her an ARIA award in 1995.

David Gulpilil from the Northern Territory became a popular film actor from 1971.

This mural at South Kempsey Primary School, NSW, was designed by famous artist Robert Campbell Junior, one of many Aboriginal painters whose works hang in galleries around the world. He combined Central Australian and Western techniques with local themes and colour. The building is the Aboriginal resource centre and was formerly the schoolhouse at Burnt Bridge mission.

Political Developments From the 1980s

Aboriginal initiative accelerated strongly from the 1970s and 1980s. Direct action continued and became more common and gradually more sophisticated, from strikes and demonstrations. Demonstrations at the Brisbane Commonwealth Games in 1982 were brave. The Bicentenary March in Sydney on Australia Day 1988 was impressively organized and massively supported. The sheer number of new leaders and the level of their specialized skills were outstanding aspects of the scene from the 1980s. In 1984 Charles Perkins became the first Aboriginal to head a federal department. Aborigines took full advantage of opportunities given by governments, including ATSIC from 1989 to 2005, when it was abolished.

In 1986, Ernie Bridge became the first Aboriginal cabinet minister in the country, in the Western Australian state Labor government, as Minister for Aboriginal Affairs. Finally in 1998, a second Aboriginal federal parliamentarian was elected, Senator Aiden Ridgeway for the Democrats. Hyacinth Tungatalum was prominent in Northern Territory politics in the 1970s. Other emerging leaders included Margaret Valadian, Paul Hughes, Colin Bourke and Eric Willmot in education, Galarrwuy Yunupingu and Pat Dodson in land rights, Lowitja (formerly Lois) O'Donoghue and Charles Perkins in economic development, Pat O'Shane in the law, and Naomi Mayers in health. In 1996, the first Aboriginal judge, Bob Bellear, was appointed in New South Wales.

The use of courts and of the Western-style legal process also increased. The most famous cases were the Gove case of 1970–71, Coe v. Commonwealth of Australia in 1979, Mabo v. Queensland 1985–92 and the Wik case 1996. International links

Ernie Bridge, whose family had both Indigenous and First Fleet roots, became the first Aboriginal cabinet minister, in Western Australia in 1986.

Lois (later Lowitja) O'Donoghue, pictured in 1985 as Australian of the Year, was raised in a mission home, having been placed there by her father. She was the first Aboriginal nurse in South Australia and first chairperson of ATSIC in 1990.

were established with indigenous peoples elsewhere in the world, especially in north America and the Pacific, for example, participation in the World Council of Indigenous People in 1981 and the International Year of Indigenous People in 1993. By 2007, 42 per cent of the land in the Northern Territory was Aboriginal-owned.

Diversity of views and activities increased within the Aboriginal community. This has been shown by the fact that some Aborigines have opposed land rights on religious grounds ('sacred sites' belong to paganism) or social grounds (they prefer to integrate in white society) or on the grounds that they will not do much practically

Gatjil Djerrkura from Yirrkala, NT, churchman and businessman, became second Chairperson of ATSIC in 1996.

to improve material or social conditions. Link-Up, founded around 1980 in New South Wales, began to assist Aboriginal people who had been taken from their families and fostered or adopted out or raised in institutions to find their Aboriginal families. The movement rapidly spread across the country.

There was continued growth in Aboriginal participation in education. School completion rates increased from 8.6 per cent in the early 1970s to 33 per cent by 2000. By 2001, there were nearly 58,046 Aboriginal students enrolled in vocational education and

Disk jockey at the Indigenous radio station in Alice Springs, NT, run by CAAMA (the Central Australian Aboriginal Media Association), in 1993.

training courses, 7342 Aboriginal university students and 199 Aboriginal academic staff in universities. In thirty years from the early 1970s to 2000, the proportion of home ownership increased from 24 per cent to 33 per cent. Health improved patchily. Overall, though there were significant improvements in aspects of health including infant mortality, life expectancy did not increase very much between 1981 and 2001 and was still approximately twenty years below the general rate. In 1991 the Royal Commission into Aboriginal Deaths in Custody reported that Aboriginal people were imprisoned at a rate 29 times that of other Australians. From the 1990s, the rate declined but remained significantly higher than the general rate.

Problems With Self-Determination

From the late 1990s, some Aboriginal voices began to question some of the unintended consequences of self-management, especially in remote communities, in some of which problems like domestic violence, sexual abuse, drug-taking, alcoholism and petrol-sniffing were rife. Some communities attempted to restrict access to alcohol in order to help protect their women and children from violence and poverty. Sometimes this was prevented because it was seen as discriminatory or paternalistic. Where it was tried, it had mixed success. History and law graduate, Noel Pearson from Cape York, became very vocal on the need for new approaches. He and others were critical of dependence on welfare and government subsidies, urging Aboriginal people and communities to take personal responsibility and get involved in the business sector and home-ownership. In 2006, a summit meeting of Aboriginal leaders was held to discuss how to improve dysfunctional remote communities. The cities were not trouble-free, either, with a shocking riot in 2004 in the Sydney suburb of Redfern after the death of an Aboriginal youth on a bicycle who thought the police were chasing him.

In 2007, the Northern Territory report, *Little Children Are Sacred*, found horrendous levels of child abuse, particularly in some remote communities. The report triggered an urgent intervention from the federal government, on an unprecedented scale, to address health, welfare and housing conditions. The intervention was welcomed in some Aboriginal quarters but condemned in others as heavy-handed, discriminatory and paternalistic. After the change in federal government in November 2007, the intervention was maintained, even though some aspects of it were toned down. Indigenous opinion wavered, with some communities appreciating the health benefits at least. Indigenous Professor Marcia Langton of Melbourne University pointed to the need to control alcohol and to reverse welfare dependence. Many Aboriginal leaders continued to condemn the heavy-handedness and the infringement of civil rights involved.

The issues and fears of the 1970s have not been solved but they have been addressed — and have also changed. The distinction between conservative and radical blacks has blurred as young radicals to some extent mellowed with age, older leaders retired or died and a new and larger generation of leaders emerged which is more educated, skilled, independent-minded and practical. As we have seen, Aborigines have gradually increased their involvement in the formulation and implementation of Aboriginal policy. By the 21st century, Indigenous leaders had considerable control, especially at local level. Divisions between black and white continue, but their nature has changed. There remains great variety between states, regions, cities, country towns, outback reserves and within Aboriginal communities. There are great disparities in health and opportunities between those in isolated communities compared with the majority now living in towns and cities. What is clear is that Aboriginal progress is no longer solely dependent on the goodwill of whites; it has built up enough momentum to overcome backlashes. There was a great outpouring of emotion from both Indigenous and non-indigenous Australians attending the parliamentary apology to the 'Stolen Generations' in February 2008. Some saw in this a sign of either closure or a new beginning or both. But others demanded monetary compensation. One critic of the 'intervention', Galarrwuy Yunupingu of Yirrkala, told his family in 2008 that 'no government, no politician, no journalist or TV man, no priest, no greenie, no well-meaning dreamer from the city is going to put your life right for you'.

READING 7

Land Rights

Australia Day 1972 was a most significant day for the Aboriginal rights movement. An Aboriginal Embassy was set up on the lawn of Parliament House, Canberra, to the profound embarrassment of the government. Following are the embassy's Five Points:

We demand –

1. Full State rights to the Northern Territory under Aboriginal ownership and control with all titles to minerals, etc.
2. Ownership of all other reserves and settlements throughout Australia with all titles to minerals and mining rights.
3. The preservation of all sacred lands not included in Points 1 and 2.
4. Ownership of certain areas of certain cities with all titles to minerals and mining rights.
5. As compensation, an initial payment of six billion dollars for all other land throughout Australia plus a percentage of the gross national product per annum.

READING 8

Aboriginal Despair in the 1970s

The plight of detribalized Aborigines is expressed in this short poem which appeared in *New Dawn*, February 1974.

> ABORIGINES
> We are few, but we were great.
> Our tribes were scattered
> Unlike our heritage torn and battered
> We drink, we gamble, we've lost our respect.
> Our children scattered in schools and out-numbered by whites,
> Sometimes feared, sometimes rejected, sometimes accepted,
> Never go on Walk-about anymore
> Our ancestors angry, our Dream-time left out.
> Who are we? the quarter-and half-caste.

Janette Forrest, age 16

READING 9

Aboriginal Hope in the 1980s

This is a speech delivered in January 1984 by Charles Perkins, secretary of the federal Department of Aboriginal Affairs.

Tomorrow we celebrate Australia Day, but what does Australia Day mean to Australians?

To some it is an excuse for a holiday. To many others it is another meaningful move towards nationhood and, possibly, a republic.

It becomes a time to reflect on our traditions, history and national consciousness.

The message for all is national pride and achievement. There is no doubt much has been achieved in Australia, but for whom? Australia is a healthy, prosperous country with a stable political system, a low inflation rate and a huge Gross National Product.

There is no doubt Australia has made it. Australians can be justifiably proud.

However, this is only one side of the coin.

The other side is the dark side.

This is the turbulent, unhappy and embarrassing side of the Australian national scene.

THE FACE OF INJUSTICE

This is the side which reveals the 200-year history of white/black relations in this country. It began with Captain Cook's arrival and it continues today …

The granting of land rights will help provide a base for the restoration of our society, economically and socially.

It will give us a psychological boost, restoring our pride.

It is the first rung on a very long ladder.

From this should follow the re-establishment of a healthy, well-housed, self-managing race of people able and willing to contribute to the harmonious progress of Australia as Australians …

Let us leave a legacy of hope for our children.

We belong to each other and we cannot let the past haunt our present and future. We must create together the kind of society where differences of culture are accepted, where disadvantage for any section is not acceptable be it women, the aged, ethnic groups or Aborigines.

The future is ours to create. Let us not live through the trauma of America and England.

Let history teach us something.

QUESTIONS FOR READINGS 7 TO 9

What views of the Aboriginal past are held by the writers of the three readings?

What views of the Aboriginal future do they hold?

How realistic were they? Do they reflect change within the Aboriginal community?

READING 10

The Barunga Statement, 1988

We, the Indigenous owners and occupiers of Australia, call on the Australian Government and people to recognize our rights:

- to self-determination and self-management, including the freedom to pursue our own economic, social, religious and cultural development;
- to permanent control and enjoyment of our ancestral lands;
- to compensation for the loss of use of our lands, there having been no extinction of original title;
- to protection of and control of access to our sacred sites, sacred objects, artefacts, designs, knowledge and works of art;
- to the return of the remains of our ancestors for burial in accordance with our traditions;
- to respect for and promotion of our Aboriginal identity, including the cultural, linguistic, religious and historical aspects, and including the right to be educated in our own languages and in our own culture and history;
- in accordance with the universal declaration of human rights, the international covenant on economic, social and cultural rights, the international covenant on civil and political rights, and the international convention on the elimination of all forms of racial discrimination, rights to life, liberty, security of person, food, clothing, housing, medical care, education and employment opportunities, necessary social services and other basic rights.

We call on the Commonwealth to pass laws providing:

- A national elected Aboriginal and Islander organization to oversee Aboriginal and Islander affairs;
- A national system of land rights;
- A police and justice system which recognizes our customary laws and frees us from discrimination and any activity which may threaten our identity or security, interfere with our freedom of expression or association, or otherwise prevent our full enjoyment and exercise of universally recognized human rights and fundamental freedoms.

We call on the Australian Government to support Aborigines in the development of an international declaration of principles for indigenous rights, leading to an international covenant.

And we call on the Commonwealth Parliament to negotiate with us a Treaty recognizing our prior ownership, continued occupation and sovereignty and affirming our human rights and freedom.

> Presented to Prime Minister R.J.L. Hawke at the Annual Barunga (formerly Beswick Creek, NT) cultural and sporting festival in June 1988. The Prime Minister said that he wished to have a treaty between Aboriginal and other Australians by 1990, but this did not happen.
> *Source:* http://www.austlii.edu.au/au/orgs/car/docrec/policy/brief/attach.htm

QUESTIONS FOR READING 10

Compare this document with Reading 7 on p. 99. How had Aboriginal demands changed since 1972?

Compare this document with Reading 22, *We Call for a Treaty* (1979), pp. 159–60, below. How did the ideas of sympathetic white people compare with those of Aboriginal people?

READING 11

Noel Pearson, Cape York Aboriginal leader in the 2000s, speaks.

We have a hard road ahead of us and we have set ourselves a difficult challenge: to see if we can change the future for our currently dysfunctional society in Cape York Peninsula. To see if we can change direction so that our people can rise up in the world, a world where our current position is at the lowest and most miserable bottom end.

The first part of the journey down this difficult road, was to get our thinking straight. Across the full range of policy thinking about our people's affairs, there are ruling nostrums that are fatally flawed. Some of the misconceptions are subtle — but profoundly decisive. I will quickly reiterate some examples of this wrong thinking:

• it is true that our people are frequently victimized — *but to see ourselves as victims weakens us*, it makes our people resign themselves to continued victimization (while the fewer apparently capable people defend them as victims).

• racism is a terrible burden and impediment that our people are forced to endure — *but we must not make it our disability*, otherwise it debilitates us and succeeds in its purpose of destroying our resolve to survive and prosper as a people.

• the welfare safety net exists as a universal entitlement of all citizens — *but we don't have a right to languish at the dependent bottom end of society*, we instead have a right to a fair place in the real economy (i.e., a greater right).

• everything we do must be 'culturally appropriate' — *but in practice 'culturally appropriate' usually means substandard* in terms of quality, expectation, performance and achievement.

• it is true that the ultimate explanation of our parlous condition is our history, our dispossession and consequent trauma — *but these explanations frequently do not confer ready solutions*, other than to reiterate the responsibility of Australian society to assist our people to rise out of our problems and to take our rightful place in our country. Rather, there are more immediate explanations of our problems — passive welfare dependency, grog and drug addiction — which require, and are amenable to, practical resolution in the present.

Confronting our poor thinking will be an ongoing process. The leadership that is developing and the new thinking that is being shared and generated among community members and community leaders, is critical. This leadership must be encouraged and re-developed at the family level because that leadership did exist in earlier times — it is just that it has broken down as our problems have overwhelmed us.

Noel Pearson, 'What Cape York Communities Can Do to help themselves', posted 15 June 2001, edited version of the Hollingworth

lecture, given on 30 November 2000.
Source: Online Opinion, http://www.onlineopinion.com.au/view.
asp?article=1052

READING 12

The Inteyerrkwe Statement, 2008

We the Aboriginal males from Central Australia and our visitor brothers from around Australia gathered at Inteyerrkwe in July 2008 to develop strategies to ensure our future roles as grandfathers, fathers, uncles, nephews, brothers, grandsons, and sons in caring for our children in a safe family environment that will lead to a happier, longer life that reflects opportunities experienced by the wider community.

We acknowledge and say sorry for the hurt, pain and suffering caused by Aboriginal males to our wives, to our children, to our mothers, to our grandmothers, to our granddaughters, to our aunties, to our nieces and to our sisters.

We also acknowledge that we need the love and support of our Aboriginal women to help us move forward.

First national Aboriginal Men's Health Conference in Alice Springs, NT, July 2008. *Source:* http://www.caac.org.au/malehealthinfo/ malehealthsummit2008sorry.pdf

QUESTIONS FOR READINGS 11 AND 12

How do these approaches to Aboriginal problems differ from those of the 1970s and 1980s (Readings 7, 9 and 10)?

Does Noel Pearson imply any failings in the policy of self-determination?

How is the theme of 'taking responsibility' expressed in these extracts?

FURTHER READING

Overviews of Aboriginal responses:
Broome, R., *Aboriginal Australians: Black Responses to White Dominance, 1788–2001*, 3rd ed., Sydney: Allen & Unwin, 2002.

Flood, J.M., *The Original Australians: Story of the Aboriginal People*, Sydney: Allen & Unwin, 2006.

Land Rights:
Charlesworth, M., *The Aboriginal Land Rights Movement,* 2nd ed., Melbourne: Hodja, 1984.

Healey, Justin (ed.), *Aboriginal Land Rights*, Sydney: Spinney Press, *c.* 2002.

Loos, Noel, and Koiki Mabo, *Edward Koiki Mabo: His Life and Struggle for Land Rights*, Brisbane: University of Queensland Press, 1996.

Other issues:
Pearson, N., *Welfare Reform and Economic Development for Indigenous Communities*, Sydney: Centre for Independent Studies, 2005.

Rowley, C.D., *Recovery: The Politics of Aboriginal Reform*, Melbourne: Penguin, 1986.

Trudgen, Richard, *Why Warriors Lie Down and Die: Towards an Understanding of why the Aboriginal People of Arnhem Land Face the Greatest Crisis in Health and Education Since European Contact*, Darwin: Aboriginal Resource and Development Services Inc., 2000.

Periodicals:
Aboriginal History, from 1977.

Identity, 1971–75; *Aboriginal and Islander Identity*, 1975-79; *Identity*, 1979–82.

Koori Mail, the fortnightly national Aboriginal and Torres Strait Islander newspaper, South Lismore, NSW, 1991–.

PART TWO

White Reactions to the Aborigines

8 Policy and Practice in the Colonial Period, 1788–1855

In 1788 British authority brought with it a long tradition of dealing with indigenous peoples, be they Irish, Indians, Native Americans or Africans. New South Wales, as it was then known, was a British possession and therefore all its inhabitants were British subjects, entitled to the rights and protection of British subjects, and heir to the demands of subjecthood. At any rate, this was the theory. Indeed, the instructions issued to colonial governors by the British government normally reminded governors of this, and often went on to detail a policy of peaceful co-existence involving protection and civilization and Christianization of the 'natives'.

Even assuming goodwill and consistency on the part of administrators, this was an impossible policy. Aborigines were to be protected against the aggression of white people, yet aggression itself was part of the policy of frontier expansion. Further, although policy said the Aborigines were British subjects, it also said that 'hostile incursions' by the Aborigines should be punished as if they came from a foreign state. Now, Aborigines and white settlers inevitably clashed over the possession of land. Which set of 'British subjects' would the government protect, the black or the white? Naturally, most often it was the latter. If the Aborigines were British subjects and their land British, what rights did these black subjects have to their land? Could the government wage war against its own subjects, even if they were black?

Even though well intentioned, the official policy was virtually meaningless, especially when it was applied to real crisis situations. The attitude of the governor at any particular time could determine how much respect was shown to official policy at the local level.

In the Beginning

Governor Phillip's first aim in 1788 with regard to the Aborigines was to open up amicable relations with them, to demonstrate to them the goodwill of the Europeans. As we have seen, at first the Aborigines did not want to cooperate. In fact, Phillip's advances were not merely ignored, they were forcibly repulsed; so he decided to force a beginning to the communication between white and black. Aborigines were captured, but this did not have the desired result. Phillip's brave landing at Manly backfired also; the kind-hearted and well-meaning

Arthur Phillip, the founding Governor of New South Wales, had very good intentions towards the Aboriginal people.

governor left nursing a spear wound. Phillip sensibly refused to retaliate. Finally, for no apparent reason, and certainly not because of anything Phillip had done, communication was established. It was not long before Phillip himself wrecked the happy state of affairs which he had sought, but which came about in spite of him. On 9 December 1790, Phillip's gamekeeper, a fairly disreputable convict named McIntire, was speared to death (by Pemulwuy, it was said). Phillip swore revenge, and was egged on by Bennelong who belonged to a rival clan. A punitive expedition was sent to bring in the culprits, dead or alive, but met complete failure in the alien bush.

The ambiguous policy of friendship and revenge — with a dash of indifference — continued for over a century. In notorious Tasmania, Lieutenant-Governor Collins declared in 1810 that the murder of Aborigines was as serious a crime as the murder of a 'civilized person'. The Royal Instructions to Lieutenant-Governor Stirling of Western Australia in 1829 were very similar. Murder in self-defence became an exception, however, and 'self-defence' covered a multitude of sins. Sometimes, governors felt bound to go so far against their benevolent aims as to order settlers to form vigilante groups for their self-defence, with inevitable, bloody results. When it came to the Aborigines, colonial administrators forgot nothing — and learned nothing.

There were distinct legal problems in treating Aborigines with the respect due to British subjects. If Aborigines were charged with a crime or appeared as witnesses, they could not testify effectively; this was partly because of the language barrier but, in any case, they could not testify on oath as the oath was said to bind only those who believed in the Christian God and the penalty of hell for perjurers. These problems arose only if the suspect were caught, which was sometimes impossible; catching the right man was another problem. In the case of crimes against Aborigines, the evidence problem was added to by the reluctance of one European to testify against another over the killing of a mere 'native'.

Ironically, when the official attitude was most sympathetic, the failure of the policy was most tragic. Governor Macquarie was well pleased with the racial harmony of his first few years, but around 1814–16 the Aborigines renewed their attacks. Macquarie urged restraint and began to evolve a practical program. Perhaps because of his Scottish Highland background, Macquarie was eager to find, recognize officially and strengthen tribal chiefs (even though there were none in the usual sense). To give a lead, he set up Bungaree as chief of the artificial 'Broken Bay Tribe', with metal plate around his neck, European clothes and admiral's hat, a fishing boat and gear.

Governor Lachlan Macquarie.

In 1815 Macquarie established a Native Institution to train Aboriginal youths in the habits of settled life, but even the 'successful' pupils had a habit of running off to live in the bush with their people, especially the boys. By 1823, most of the Institution's inmates had been transferred to a reserve at the 'Black Town'. (Some of the girls married ex-convicts, received land grants and were the ancestors of most of the Dharug people around Sydney today.) In 1816, Macquarie inaugurated an annual 'native feast' at Parramatta. Blankets and other goods were given out, the 'chiefs' entertained, and each year tribes from further afield joined in, from as far away as west of the Blue Mountains.

However, the governor's plan of pacifying the tribes through (fictional) chiefs and 'civilizing' the children was

Bungaree, wearing cast-off military clothing and his king-plate. He had circumnavigated Australia with Matthew Flinders in 1801–02 and was a brilliant mimic. But his consort is shown smoking and there are grog bottles nearby.

doomed from the beginning, and the Aborigines did not respond to bribery. In Tasmania, Lieutenant-Governor George Arthur made a pictorial proclamation in 1829 to convince the Aborigines of equal justice (see the cover illustration). He was equally sympathetic, and equally unrealistic, in his plan for native reserves. In Western Australia, within five years of the founding of the colony, the Battle of Pinjarra had cost up to 30 black lives.

The Crisis of Authority

In the 1830s and 1840s, the influence of the evangelical humanitarians was at its height and the British government at that time was taking a strong line for the protection of the persons and rights of 'native peoples'. Unfortunately for Australia's Aborigines, this was one of the greatest periods of expansion of the frontier (and, therefore, of frontier conflict) and so, official good intentions and the self-interest of settlers were in sharp conflict. The Aborigines, in the middle, remained the losers.

The period of Governor Sir George Gipps (1838–46) was a vital one, with all the issues raised very clearly and all parties in the conflict drawn up in battle array. The policy Gipps tried to put into practice was basically the same as those of other colonies: Victoria was not separated from New South Wales until 1851, and Western Australia (1829) and South Australia (1836) had similar aims for the Aborigines.

A major part in the new policy was played by a Protectorate of the Aborigines. In New South

George Augustus Robinson, the 'Conciliator' in Tasmania, poses as a Victorian gentleman. (Photo by W.P. Dowling)

Wales, the local Commissioners for Crown Lands were given the additional job of Protectors of Aborigines in 1839. In Tasmania, George Augustus Robinson was Protector. South Australia established a Protectorate in 1837, with a permanent Protector in 1838. In the southern part of New South Wales later called Victoria, the most complete system was set up in 1838, with Robinson from Tasmania as Chief Protector and four district protectors. These protectors had to befriend and protect the Aborigines and persuade them to 'settle down'. Full cooperation was extended to missionaries, for Christianization was considered a most important part of civilization.

Sir George Gipps, Governor of New South Wales, 1838–46.

Governor Gipps was faced in his first year with a major racial crisis, one which was regarded by him, by the 'idealists' and by the 'realists' alike, as something of a test case for the government's hard line on Aboriginal rights. In June 1838 at the Myall Creek station of Henry Dangar, in the Bingara district of north-western New South Wales, eleven convict and

A sketch depicting the Myall Creek massacre in June 1838. (C. Pelham, *The Chronicle of Crime; or, the Newgate Calendar*, Vol. 1, London, 1841)

ex-convict workers, led by a free man, killed at least 28 Aborigines and burned their bodies. The victims were not associated with any case of cattle-spearing. Unfortunately for the culprits, a number of unusual circumstances combined to bring them to justice. Two white witnesses reported the incident despite social pressure against their action; the magistrate, Edward Denny Day, listened, investigated thoroughly and passed on the evidence to higher authority, and that higher authority took action to prosecute the murderers.

Gipps, backed by the strong line of the Colonial Office, was blessed with a dedicated and hard-working Attorney-General, John Hubert Plunkett, who prosecuted the Myall Creek culprits in a most determined manner. To achieve his aim, Plunkett overcame a number of problems: two trials, the loyalty of the accused to each other, the disallowing of the testimony of an Aboriginal called Davey, and a vigorous campaign by various squatters and the *Sydney Herald* to have the accused men acquitted. Finally, however, seven of the men were found guilty and hanged in December 1838.

On the one side of the controversy were the 'realists' (the squatters and their sympathizers), who had a lot to lose if Aborigines' rights were enforced. They claimed that if the Myall Creek men were executed it would encourage Aborigines all over the country to try to get away with more violence. They claimed that they also needed protection, against the Aborigines. The murderers themselves, who may well have acted with at least the permission of their employers, never denied their guilt but could not understand why there was such fuss over the death of Aborigines.

On the other side, humanitarians in the colony were outraged by both the massacre and the fact that 'respectable' squatters, lawyers and publishers could support murderers. The clergymen J.D. Lang, J. Saunders and L.E. Threlkeld and journalists including Henry Parkes, E.S. Hall and W.A. Duncan fought just as hard for the view that murder was murder whatever the colour of the victims. The text of nearly all sermons in Sydney churches on the Sunday before the verdict was Acts 17:26, '[God] hath made of one blood all nations of men for to dwell on all the face of the earth'. The point was even made that Aboriginal resistance was based rightly on resentment at the loss of their land.

With the executions, it could be said that the governor, the official policy and humanitarian concern had won a victory. Certainly, it encouraged the governor to press on with his policy in some new directions and it put the squatters on their guard. But in the long run it was a hollow victory and a costly one. The angry public reaction and other problems made the authorities reluctant to pursue a similar case shortly after, especially with stories arriving of massacres of white settlers on the frontier. Gipps' attempt to allow Aboriginal evidence in court passed the Legislative Council in 1839, but was vetoed by London for technical legal reasons. About a decade later it was rejected again, although adopted successfully in South Australia. The governor's attempts to restrict frontier expansion, and therefore violence, failed.

In 1839 the Border Police force was set up to make protection more effective. However, the small number and poor quality of these police, the extent of the frontier and the uncooperative attitude of many squatters made this step almost useless as far as the Aborigines were concerned. A Bill to forbid Aborigines' carrying firearms was disallowed, but in 1838 the sale of alcohol to Aborigines was banned, but not very effectively.

One very unfortunate consequence of the Myall Creek affair was that murders of Aborigines did not so much decline as become more secret: poisoning the flour that Aborigines might steal and eat allegedly became more common than shootings.

It was not long before most of the colonial Aboriginal policy was looking very shaky. The Port Phillip District (Victoria) Protectorate was never realistic; it was 'in the way' of the general trend of overall government policy, which involved the dispossession of Aborigines in favour of sheep and cattle. Whites were more hostile to the Protectorate, because the plan included the setting up of small reserves for Aborigines on some of the best land.

There were some minor successes, but the Aboriginal response was not encouraging, a number of district Protectors resigned within a

John Batman made a treaty with the 'chiefs' of the Kulin to 'buy' 600,000 acres around the area of Melbourne in 1835. The government invalidated the sale because it regarded the land as the property of the Crown.

short time and Chief Protector Robinson was particularly ineffective. The Protectorate was finally wound up in 1849, but had been almost defunct by 1839. Governor Hutt of Western Australia appointed Guardians of Aborigines and though this similar arrangement lasted longer than Victoria's Protectorate, it was just as ineffective as far as the Aborigines were concerned.

Christian Missions
The 1840s also saw the failure of most of the Christian missions to the Aborigines, a failure so complete that it was over a generation before most churches tried again. The Wesleyan Methodists were involved in a number of short-lived ventures in the 1820s. One of these, near Wellington, NSW, was taken over in 1831 by the Anglicans' Church Missionary Society for eleven years. It lasted as a privately run, government-aided mission until the 1850s. The Presbyterians

sponsored a station at Nundah near Brisbane, which was run by German missionaries from 1838 to 1845; they also supported an itinerant worker in the far north-west of New South Wales, the Rev. William Ridley, who became an authority on Aboriginal languages. In the 1840s there was a short-lived Roman Catholic mission on Stradbroke Island. In what later became Victoria, there were two independent ventures in the Melbourne area, from 1837 to 1839, and from 1845 to 1851, as well as a Wesleyan Methodist mission at Buntingdale for ten years from 1838.

In some ways the most interesting mission was that of the Rev. L.E. Threlkeld at Lake Macquarie, NSW, from 1825 to 1841. In the early years, there was a heated controversy on missionary strategy between the pioneer 'flogging parson', the Rev. Samuel Marsden (later missionary to New Zealand) and Threlkeld. Marsden believed that the Aborigines would have to be civilized or Europeanized before they could be made into Christians. To him, Christianity and his own culture were, in practical terms, inseparable. Threlkeld, on the other hand, strove to understand the Aborigines, their language and way of life. In order to present the Christian faith to them in their own language, he translated St Luke's gospel into Awabagal. Unfortunately for him, in the short term, his mission was just as much a failure as others. It was recognized later, however, that Threlkeld's strategy was the right one and that, in fact, with its emphasis on cooperation and sharing, Aboriginal traditional society came closer in some ways to the Christian ideal than did European society.

The only mission to last

The Rev. Samuel Marsden, senior chaplain of New South Wales, founder of the New Zealand Maori mission and critic of Lancelot Threlkeld's missionary strategy with the Awabagal. (Engraving by Richard Woodman, 1835).

continuously from the early colonial period to modern times was the New Norcia mission north of Perth, founded in 1846 by Roman Catholic Benedictine monks form Spain.

Aborigines and the Economy

African missionaries such as David Livingstone saw Christianity and commerce as partners in 'civilizing' native races. Less was done officially to encourage Aborigines into commerce than was done to spread Christianity, but governments sometimes promoted the view that Aborigines should enter the white economy — and society — through employment as various kinds of labourers.

For a long time the pastoral industry was the only one that could employ many Aborigines; and even in this industry in the colonial years, most stock-owners were unwilling to allow Aborigines to do more than odd jobs. There were exceptions, however, especially during the gold rushes, which took away white workers. Aboriginal skills and the Aboriginal way of life made working with horses, sheep and cattle more attractive than other jobs, so that on the station of a sympathetic squatter during the gold rushes, it was usual to find some Aboriginal workers. In western Victoria, for example, Thomas Chirnside employed about twenty Aborigines in sheep-washing in the 1850s. The experience in the 1850s of E.D.S. Ogilvie of the upper Clarence River, NSW, was that European immigrants were likely to desert his station for the goldfields, Chinese were unreliable and Aborigines, if well treated, were good workers. To this day, on the frontier, the Aboriginal has been the mainstay of the cattle industry.

Other avenues of employment for Aborigines in the first half of the nineteenth century included the sealing industry in Bass Strait, prostitution and the police forces. As in the cattle and sheep industries, these forms of employment generally exploited Aborigines as 'cheap labour'. Nevertheless, it cannot be denied that this aspect of colonial policy toward the Aborigines — their employment and participation in the money economy — failed, at least in the short term.

The Colonial Legacy

By the time the six Australian colonies had received self-government (most in the 1850s), Aboriginal policy was in tatters. This situation was largely the result of both the contradictions in the policy itself and the fact that Aborigines preferred to use parts of that policy for their own purposes and not in the way expected by the whites. For instance, they patronized the few schools on offer only to the extent that, and for as long as, they found it useful to do so. This sort of thing made white policy-makers and administrators doubt whether the Aborigines could ever be civilized.

There were some aspects of colonial policy which survived. One of them was the annual distribution of blankets, normally on the Queen's birthday. Governor Gipps was inclined to do away with the blanket issue, as he felt it tended to make the Aborigines lazy and too dependent on charity. Ironically perhaps, the squatters, who had once opposed gifts of blankets, changed their minds after a time and Governor Sir Charles FitzRoy reintroduced regular blanket distribution. So, when the colonies became self-governing, distribution of blankets (and other goods) was the major feature of Aboriginal policy, such as it was. Another unfortunate continuing element was the use of police in dealings with Aboriginal people, a practice which helped to establish deep and long-lasting ill-feeling between the two groups.

Another aspect of colonial policy that survived self-government, notably in Queensland, was the use of Aborigines as troopers on the frontier: the Native Mounted Police. The original idea was that police discipline and pride in the uniform would educate and civilize young Aboriginal recruits and it was also thought that the force would actually be useful on the frontier. Native Police forces were, however, far more effective in the pacification of hostile frontier tribes than they were in the civilization of the Aboriginal troopers. The troopers were always recruited from outside the areas where it was intended to use them. Often 'foreign' Aborigines had even less feeling for local tribesmen than had white people, and the troopers tended to regard their duties as a good way of obtaining women and other valuable 'things', and

Five troopers of the Queensland Native Mounted Police with their officer in about 1870.

of punishing their traditional enemies. The Native Police, as always under European leadership, lasted in Victoria only from 1842 to 1853, but in Queensland until 1909

By the middle of the nineteenth century it was quite widely thought that the Aborigines were doomed to extinction, that something in their contact with European life mysteriously caused them to decline more quickly than one would expect, taking into consideration the small proportion deliberately killed by whites.

There was some grim evidence for this from Tasmania where, by the time of self-government, the Tasmanians were almost extinct. There had been brutal massacres, but even the most benevolent protective measures taken by humanitarians like Governor Arthur and G.A. Robinson seemed to accelerate the decline of the Tasmanian Aborigines. The notorious Black Line of 1830, intended to round up Aborigines for their own protection, merely accelerated the process it was intended to stop because they were resettled on Flinders Island where they were almost wiped out by disease. The failure of good intentions in turn reinforced the general feeling of hopelessness even amongst friends of the Aborigines. The scene was set for decades of apathy and neglect.

READING 13

The European Takeover
The rationale for the takeover of Australia by Britain was well expressed by Mr Justice Blackburn in his judgement on the Yirrkala (Gove) land rights case in 1971.

> There is a principle which was a philosophical justification for the colonization of the territory of less civilized peoples: that the whole earth was open to the industry and enterprise of the human race, which had a duty and the right to develop the earth's resources. The more advanced peoples were, therefore, justified in dispossessing, if necessary, the less advanced.

> Milirrpum and Others v. Nabalco Pty Ltd and the Commonwealth of Australia, Supreme Court of the Northern Territory, 1971.

READING 14

The Aboriginal Policy of the Colonial Government
The benevolent intentions of colonial policy are shown by the following extracts here and in Reading 15 from instructions to governors from Secretaries of State for the Colonies.
  Governor Phillip's instructions (25th April 1787):

> You are to endeavour by every possible means to open an intercourse with the natives, and to conciliate their affections, enjoining all our subjects to live in amity and kindness with them. And, if any of our subjects wantonly destroy them, or give them any unnecessary interruption in the exercise of their several occupations, it is our will and pleasure that you do cause such offenders to be brought to punishment according to the degree of the offence. You will endeavour to produce an account of the numbers inhabiting the neighbourhood of the intended settlement, and report your opinion to one of our Secretaries of State in what manner our intercourse with these people may be turned to the advantage of this colony.

> *Historical Records of Australia*, Series I, Vol.1.

READING 15

The Aboriginal Policy of the Colonial Government
Governor Darling's instructions (17 July 1825) were as follows:

> And it is Our further Will and Pleasure that you do, to the utmost of your power, promote Religion and Education among the Native Inhabitants of Our said Colony, or of the Lands and Islands thereto adjoining; and that you do especially take care to protect them in their persons, and in the free enjoyment of their possessions; and that you do by all lawful means prevent and restrain all violence and injustice, which may in any manner be practised or attempted against them; and that you take such measures as may appear to you with the advice of Our said Archdeacon to be necessary for their conversion to the Christian Faith and for their advancement in Civilization.
>
> *Historical Records of Australia*, Series I, Vol. 12.

READING 16

Conciliation Between Aborigines and Whites
Edward Ogilvie was a pastoralist on the upper Clarence River, NSW, from the 1840s. Following are extracts from a letter he wrote to the *Sydney Morning Herald* in July 1842.

> Since the hostile encounters with the blacks which took place upon this river about a year ago in consequence of the murders committed by them, they have rarely shown themselves, but have kept among the mountains, and avoided all intercourse, always making off as fast as possible if accidentally seen, though they have occasionally crept unobserved upon the huts, and carried off the shepherds' blankets and axes.

(Finally, helped by his knowledge of their language, Ogilvie managed to 'bring them to a parley'.)

> We said that we had made war upon them because they had killed white people, but that now our anger was gone and that we wished to live in

peace with them; that we wanted nothing in their country but the grass, and would leave them their kangaroos, their opossums, and their fish. Toolbillibam here interposed, to know if we would not leave them their honey also. We assured him that it was quite at his service, and that he might make himself perfectly easy about rats, bandicoots, grubs and all other small game. All this appeared extremely satisfactory to our audience. We told them that if they would not rob or injure our people, nor kill our sheep, that no person would harm them; but, on the contrary, would give them bread when they came to the stations; and we promised that if they conducted themselves peaceably for a time, that we would give each of them a tomahawk. We pointed out to them the direction of all our stations and told them when they visited them, not to sneak from three to tree, but to walk up openly and call out to give notice of their approach, and put their weapons out of their hands — all this they promised to attend to. The sun was now sinking; therefore, after distributing amongst them our pocket knives, our handkerchiefs, and such articles of our dress as we could spare, we told them we must go. They all rose and accompanied us to the camp, which lay in our route. Toolbillibam walked before and with much care parted the long grass with his hands and cleared away all obstacles from our path …

The only apology I can offer for occupying so large a portion of your valuable space, is that, without entering into the details, I could not have attained the object I had in view, namely, to show the very placable disposition and unrevengeful spirit of these people, and to convince those who are in the habit of looking upon them as little better than wild beasts, that they are mistaken.

READING 17

Attitudes to the Aborigines in the Colonial Period

In *The Last of the Tasmanians*, James Bonwick writes of attitudes in colonial Tasmania.

The editor of a Wellington paper writes: 'We have ourselves heard "old hands" declare to the common practice of shooting them [Aborigines] to supply food for dogs.' He had heard of the employment of poisoned rum. Such conduct was manifested from the very settlement of the colony ...

The public sentiment appears to have been either one of indifference toward the Natives, or that of direct antipathy. Many sympathized too much in the feeling of the man who said, 'I'd as leave shoot 'em as so many sparrows'. Even Captain Stokes was forced to write: 'Such is the perversion of feeling among the colonists, that they cannot conceive that any one can sympathize with the Black race as their fellow-men'. In any early proclamation, Governor Sorell thus records his condemnation of such treatment: 'Cruelties have been perpetrated upon the Aborigines repugnant to humanity, and disgraceful to the British character; whilst few attempts can be traced on the part of the colonist, to conciliate the Natives, or to make them sensible that peace and forbearance were the objects desired'.

J. Bonwick, *The Last of the Tasmanians,* London, 1870,, pp. 58, 59.

READING 18

Attitudes to the Aborigines in the Colonial Period

Attitudes could change on closer inspection, however. Watkin Tench wrote the following in the 1790s.

With the natives we were very little acquainted ... on our arrival in the country. Our intercourse with them was neither frequent or cordial. They seemed studiously to avoid us, either from fear, jealousy, or hatred. When they met with unarmed stragglers, they sometimes killed, and sometimes wounded them. I confess that, in common with many others, I was inclined to attribute this conduct, to a spirit of malignant levity. But a farther acquaintance with them, founded on several instances of their humanity and generosity ... has entirely reversed my opinion; and led me to conclude, that the unprovoked outrages committed upon them, by unprincipled individuals among us, caused the evils we had experienced. To prevent them from being plundered of their fishing-tackle and weapons of war, a proclamation was issued, forbidding their sale among us; but it was not attended with the good effect which was hoped for from it.

W. Tench, *A Complete Account of the Settlement at Port Jackson in New South Wales*, London, 1793, p. 4.

QUESTIONS FOR READINGS 13 TO 18

Was it right for Europeans to take over the land of Australia?

Did the colonial governors make a genuine effort to fulfil their instructions about treatment of the Aborigines?

What was Edward Ogilvie's opinion of the Aborigines (Reading 16)?

How accurately does James Bonwick picture Europeans' attitudes to Aborigines in Reading 17?

Was Watkin Tench unusual in his attitudes?

How much effect did the attitudes of individual Europeans have on Aboriginal-European relations overall?

FURTHER READING

Hasluck, P.M.C., *Black Australians: A Survey of Native Policy in Western Australia, 1829–1897*, Melbourne: Melbourne University Press, 1942, 1970.

Reece, R.H.W., *Aborigines and Colonists: Aborigines and Colonial Society in New South Wales in the 1830s and 1840s*, Sydney: Sydney University Press, 1974.

Reynolds, H. (ed.), *Dispossession: Black Australians and White Invaders*, Sydney: Allen & Unwin, 1989.*

Reynolds, H., *This Whispering in Our Hearts*, Sydney: Allen & Unwin, 1998.

Woolmington, J. (ed.), *Aborigines in Colonial Society: 1788–1850 — From 'Noble Savage' to 'Rural Pest'*, Melbourne: Cassell, 1973.*

* These are collections of documents.

9 The Protection Era, 1855-1937

From self-government until the Second World War, government policy towards the Aborigines was such that it could be described by one authority as a policy which aimed 'to smooth the pillow of a dying race'. This was the period of a new kind of protection policy, only this time it was protection without protectors.

As the frontier extended, in Queensland, Western Australia and Central Australia, the same questions faced in Victoria and New South Wales were raised over and over again. The main issue — whether the Europeans would win the land from the original possessors — was really settled years before in the south-east. After the colonies became self-governing and until the governmental measures outlined above were enacted, neglect of the problems of the Aborigines and the frontier was almost total. The real problems were further and further removed from the 'do-gooders' in the southern cities. In this period of official neglect much was left to private individuals; station-owners sometimes provided work, clothing, rations and even housing for the local Aborigines.

The police force seems always to have had a peculiar relationship with Aborigines all over the country. In New South Wales, where blanket distribution was almost all there was left of Aboriginal policy, the police doubled as Aboriginal 'welfare' officers. Being dependent paupers was bad enough, but being dependent on the agents of an oppressive alien law was even more degrading.

In Queensland, of course, there was also the Native Mounted Police. Rather than protect white and black on the frontier, the black troopers were used to clear out other Aborigines from pastoral areas, often with brutal efficiency. On the other hand, private benevolence was shown at Mackay in the 1870s by a white settler who set up a private reserve.

The gap between colonial policy and the new protection varied from colony to colony. Victoria appointed a protection board in 1860 and an Act nine years later put the board on a firmer footing. An amending Act in 1886 extended the board's interest to 'half-castes'. In New South Wales a protector was appointed in 1881 and a protection board in 1883, but the situation was not regularized by parliament until 1909. Aboriginal policy in Western Australia was under British government control until 1897, although the local legislature passed an Aborigines Protection Act in 1886. The Western Australian Aborigines Act of 1905 was similar to the

Archibald Meston, flamboyant journalist and politician and architect of the Queensland Aborigines Protection Act in 1897.

Acts in other states. Queensland made provision for Aboriginal protection by the Aboriginals' Protection and Restriction of Sale of Opium Act of 1897, which was administered by two protectors, one for the north and one for the south. In South Australia, there was no Act for Aboriginal affairs until the Aborigines Protection Act of 1911. Tasmania saw no need for a policy as the inevitable deaths of the last 'full-blood' Tasmanians occurred in 1869 (William Lanney), 1876 (Truganini) and 1888 (Suke), and the handful of part-Tasmanians was ignored.

Protection Policies Emerge
Victoria was different — its official protection policy started soon after self-government, and had to deal with relatively fewer Aborigines over a smaller area with greater resources (Victoria was the 'gold'

colony). Not that the results of the policy were vastly different from results in other states; however, there was greater continuity of what concern there was. Though a number of stations and missions had closed by the 1860s, more were established. There were two missions run by Moravians: Ebenezer in the Wimmera, from 1850 to 1904, and Ramahyuck in Gippsland, from 1862 to 1908. Lake Tyers was run by the Anglicans from 1861 to 1908 and then by the Protection Board; Framlingham (1864–90) and Lake Condah (1867-1951) were taken over in similar manner.

Coranderrk (1864–1923) was the closest thing to a success story for the protection policy in the 1870s, as it became almost self-governing and self-supporting. The irony was that the very success of communities such as Coranderrk, Cumeroogunga (NSW) and Raukkan (SA) made them vulnerable. In the 1880s, the Victorian government expelled 'half-castes' from the settlements such as Coranderrk. This was supposedly to benefit the 'half-castes', by their absorption into the general population, but it deprived the settlements of labourers in the prime of life. Also, the agricultural success of the communities had made their land attractive to Europeans, and many reserves were reduced or abolished between 1890 and the 1950s, and the land leased or sold to European farmers.

The aims and objectives of the various protection boards' policies seem not to have been spelled out, but one aim would appear to have been to assist able-bodied Aborigines to help themselves and in the long run for the boards to do themselves out

'A curiosity in her own country', a cartoon by Phil May in *The Bulletin*, in the centenary year of 1888.

of a job (although they intended to continue caring for those Aborigines who could not care for themselves). At places like Coranderrk this was what happened, although it cannot be said the board deserved the credit. Rather, they are to be condemned for undermining their own supposed aims by crushing Aboriginal initiative through land resumptions and the new 'half-caste' policy.

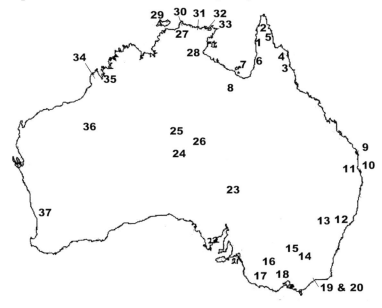

Map 5: Australia, Aboriginal missions.

1 Aurukun	14 Maloga	27 Oenpelli
2 Weipa and Mapoon	15 Warangesda	28 Roper River
3 Yarrabah	16 Ebenezer	29 Bathurst and Melville Islands
4 Hope Vale	17 Lake Condah	30 Croker and Goulburn Islands
5 Lockhart River	18 Buntingdale	31 Milingimbi
6 Mitchell River	19 Ramahyuck	32 Elcho Island
7 Mornington Island	20 Lake Tyers	33 Yirrkala
8 Doomadgee	21 Point Macleay	34 Beagle Bay
9 Fraser Island	22 Poonindie	35 Mowanjum
10 Stradbroke Island	23 Killalpaninna	36 Jigalong
11 Nundah	24 Ernabella	37 New Norcia
12 Lake Macquarie	25 Hermannsburg	
13 Wellington	26 Santa Teresa	

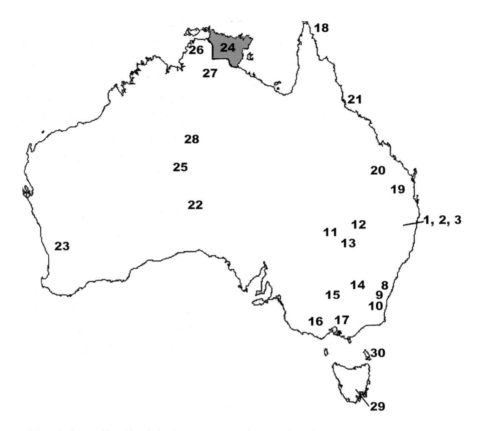

Map 6: Australia, Aboriginal reserves, stations and settlements.

1 Woodenbong
2 Tabulam
3 Cabbage Tree Island
  and Box Ridge
4 Bellbrook
5 Burnt Bridge
  and Kinchela
6 Purfleet
7 La Perouse
8 Wreck Bay
9 Bomaderry
10 Wallaga Lake

11 Angledool
12 Toomelah
13 Brewarrina
14 Cootamundra
15 Cumeroogunga
16 Framlingham
17 Coranderrk
18 Bamaga
19 Cherbourg
20 Woorabinda

21 Palm Island
22. North West Aboriginal Reserve
23 Moore River
24 Arnhem Land
25 Docker River
26 Bagot
27 Barunga (Beswick Creek)
28 Kintore
29 Oyster Bay
30 Flinders Island

In Queensland, New South Wales and to a certain extent in South Australia, private organizations began between 1870 and 1890 to exert considerable pressure which eventually led to the new protection policies in these colonies. The pressure was also practical, in that it was largely a renewed activity in Christian missions to the Aborigines which reminded governments of their responsibilities. From the 1860s, a number of unsupervised reserves in New South Wales had been set up by the government more or less of its own accord. Then a group led by Daniel Matthews and the Rev. J.B. Gribble, calling itself the Aborigines' Protection Association, set up three non-denominational mission stations: in 1874 at Maloga (later called Cumeroogunga) on the Murray River, in 1880 at Warangesda on the Murrumbidgee and in 1886 at Brewarrina on the Darling. As happened often in other colonies, the Protection Board took these over before 1900, as well as founding its own 'homes' and stations. In Queensland after 1885 a number of missions began to be established, mainly in the far north; and after the 1897 Act, the government began some settlements. In Western Australia with their Act in 1886, policy moved in a similar direction, as it did also in South Australia under the Act of 1911.

The Practice of Protection

So much for the emergence of the 'new' protective policy. How did this policy, which lasted from the second half of the nineteenth century to perhaps the middle of the twentieth, work out in practice? It has been described by some authorities as a system of 'protection-segregation': that is, separation of Aborigines in stations from white society in order to protect them from its bad effects. This applied particularly to elderly and infirm or young Aborigines, and to full-bloods rather than half-castes, but it tended to apply more and more to all Aborigines as time went by, especially in Queensland. In theory, perhaps especially in New South Wales and Victoria through places like Cumeroogunga and Coranderrk, able-bodied Aborigines were to be encouraged and instructed in how to fend for themselves. Unfortunately, whenever this began to happen, the ambitious Aboriginal found himself humbled in the face of a society which expected the worst from him and treated him accordingly, as we have seen. In its protective aspect, the policy did provide rudimentary medical care (stations often had matrons), rations, and such things as fishing tackle and agricultural implements; and blankets were still distributed.

It was a common practice to take children from communities, even from their parents, and place them with white foster families or in 'homes' or stations, if it was thought that they were 'at risk'. In this way, it was believed, that they could be salvaged from the 'primitive' life-style of their parents. This particular policy was followed across the country but particularly in the Northern Territory, Western Australia and New South Wales, and not only failed but caused heartbreak in the process, giving rise to what became known as the 'Stolen Generation'.

Education was another means of raising particularly Aboriginal children to 'civilization'. This tended to be left to the Christian missions, and in the more closely settled areas, part-Aboriginal children could go to ordinary schools. However, governments gradually became more involved in Aboriginal education as they took over or started more stations. Although, in New South Wales, Aboriginal children were supposed to attend the normal public schools, they could in practice be excluded if local white communities complained that they were not 'clean, clad and courteous'. Aboriginal pupils then required separate schools. Even when they were provided,

An Aboriginal domestic servant in Sydney in 1912. Cootamundra Girls Home in New South Wales trained many girls in domestic service after they had been taken from their families.

A family group in front of the church at Ramahyuck mission station, Gippsland, Victoria, in 1906. 'Ramahyuck' combines biblical Hebrew 'Ramah' (home) and Kurnai 'yuck' (mother or own). (Photo by H.B. Hammond)

these separate schools were never as well-equipped or well-staffed as public schools and not very suitable to Aboriginal needs.

One important but rather ineffective measure was the ban on supplying alcoholic liquor to Aborigines. Alcoholism has certainly always been a severe problem of Aboriginal health (as of Australian health in general), but it was a symptom, not a cause. It was a symptom of dispossession and exclusion.

Varieties of Protection

The personality and opinions of the man administering a state's Aboriginal policy could have quite an influence on both that policy and the way it was carried out. This is illustrated by the official attitude to 'half-castes' in Queensland and Western Australia. In Queensland, J.W. Bleakley was Chief Protector from 1913 to 1942 (followed by C. O'Leary as Director of Native Affairs from 1942 to 1963). In Western Australia, A.O. Neville was Chief Protector from 1915 to 1936 and Commissioner for Native Affairs from then until 1940.

The very existence of 'half-castes' pointed out the hypocritical attitudes of at least some whites, and was an affront to a 'moral' community, stabbing its conscience. Opinions and policies on this sensitive issue varied. Bleakley in Queensland wanted to eliminate the problem by encouraging half-castes to marry full-bloods; he sought control over all part-Aborigines, but a 1930 Act excluded those with less than a quarter Aboriginal blood. Nevertheless, he was very reluctant to exempt part-Aborigines from the control of his department, and this reluctance continued in Queensland until the 1980s. Queensland had a small number of very large government settlements to which Aboriginal families could be forcibly removed.

This desire to control 'half-castes' was shared in Western Australia, but there the policy had a different objective. The police were also heavily involved in the process of exemption. Neville saw the aim of his policy as 'protection' of full-bloods until they faded away but assisting the half-castes to be absorbed in the general (white) population. Though there were practical barriers to this policy, Neville pursued it, as is shown by the fact that much less stress was placed on Aboriginal settlements as a part of overall policy in Western Australia. Indeed, by the 1950s, there were no government stations at all. Instead, mixed-race children removed from their Aboriginal families in that state were moved into white foster homes as soon as possible. Queensland, on the other hand, placed great stress on the station or mission as the basic means of managing Aborigines, and the same was largely true also in South Australia and the Northern Territory. Thus, in essence, Western Australian policy tended to be assimilationist, while Queensland's was segregationist.

It would be fair to say that Queensland always had the closest supervision of Aborigines. For this reason, in the twentieth century

The gates of Cherbourg in 1947, one of the large institutional Aboriginal communities used in Queensland to segregate and control Aborigines.

very few of them remained between Brisbane and the New South Wales border because many from that area had moved to New South Wales stations and towns where they were left more to themselves. In New South Wales, the board tended to make already existing Aboriginal settlements into reserves and stations rather than to create stations and

'Westralian Blacks — how they are treated.' A serious representation of contemporary stories of ill-treatment as well as an ironic comment on the proposed White Australia policy. (Vincent, *The Bulletin*, 1901)

move people in from elsewhere as happened in Queensland and Western Australia. New South Wales had a far larger number of these communities, but of smaller size and less tribal diversity. 'Fringe-dwellers' were, and are, a feature of many country towns throughout Australia, but fringe-dwelling was on a smaller scale where, as in Queensland, there was a vigorous policy of herding Aborigines into institutions.

'Fringe' communities as well as mission and station communities were regarded as sources of cheap labour mainly, but not only, in the

pastoral areas of northern Australia. As late as the 1950s in a quite closely settled part of New South Wales, Aboriginal workers could be paid in alcohol or given a mere couple of pounds a week. The Aboriginal stockman became vital to the northern cattle barons. But it was only in 1968 that equal wages were granted.

Even well-meaning official policies could sometimes be frustrated by the prejudice of local white communities. In 1912, the whites of Beverley in Western Australia did not want Aborigines in the same school as their children. The same objection was raised frequently in New South Wales in the same era. In the 1920s the Progress Associations of North and South Lismore, NSW, were each sure that Aboriginal housing ought to be located in the other's half of the city.

J.W. Bleakley dominated Aboriginal policy in Queensland from 1913 to 1942 and advised the federal government on the Northern Territory.

Enter the Commonwealth

In 1911 the Commonwealth government entered the field of Aboriginal policy. The Constitution made Aborigines a state responsibility, but in 1911 the Northern Territory, with its large Aboriginal population, was transferred from South Australia to the Commonwealth. Until the Second World War, policy in the Territory tended to continue as before. The police were important here also as part-time protectors, though from 1927 to 1939, the Chief Medical Officer was part-time administrator of Aboriginal policy. In the emphasis on supervision and on the use of government and mission stations, and in the few exemptions granted to Aborigines who could look after themselves, the policy of the Northern Territory until 1930 resembled that of Queensland. This was partly because of the influence of advice from J.W. Bleakley. However, along with other factors, the involvement of the Commonwealth government was eventually to lead to reconsideration of Aboriginal policy across the whole country.

READING 19

Protection-Segregation Policies
Between 1860 and 1939, the Aboriginal policy of all the colonies (or states) operated under similar Aboriginal 'Protection Acts'. Following are extracts from Victoria's Aborigines Act of 1915.

4.   The term 'half-caste' whenever it occurs in this Act includes as well as half-castes all other persons whatever of mixed aboriginal blood; but when used elsewhere than in this and the next succeeding section the term shall unless the context requires a different meaning be read and construed as excluding such half-castes as under the provisions of this Act are to be deemed to be aboriginals.

5.   The following persons shall be deemed to be aboriginals within the meaning of this Act:–

(i)   Every aboriginal native of Victoria;

(ii)   Every half-caste who habitually associating and living with an aboriginal within the meaning of this section completed the thirty-fourth year of his or her age prior to the first day of January One thousand eight hundred and eighty-seven;

(iii)   Every female half-caste who had prior to the date aforesaid been married to an aboriginal within the meaning of this section, and was at the date aforesaid living with such aboriginal;

(iv) Every infant unable to earn his or her own living, the child of an aboriginal within the meaning of this section, living with such aboriginal;

(v) Any half-caste other than is hereinbefore specified who for the time being holds a licence in writing from the Board under regulations to be made in that behalf to reside upon any place prescribed as a place where any aboriginal or any tribe of aboriginals may reside.

6.   The Governor in Council may make regulations and orders: –

(i) For prescribing the place where any aboriginal or any tribe of aboriginals shall reside:

(ii) For prescribing terms on which contracts for and on behalf of aboriginals may be made with persons other than aboriginals, and upon which certificates may be granted to aboriginals who may be able and willing to earn a living by their own exertions:

(iii) For apportioning amongst aboriginals the earnings of aboriginals under any contract, or where aboriginals are located on a reserve the net produce of the labour of such aboriginals …

(v) For the care custody and education of the children of aboriginals …

(vii) For prescribing the conditions on which the Board may license any half-castes to reside and be maintained upon the place or places aforesaid ... and for limiting the period of such residence and for regulating the removal or dismissal of any of such persons from any such place or places:

(viii) For prescribing the conditions on which half-castes may obtain and receive assistance to enable them ... to select acquire hold enjoy and be possessed of any such Crown lands for any estate or interest therein, and the nature and amount of such assistance...

11.   All bedding clothing and other articles issued or distributed to the aboriginals by or by the direction of the said Board shall be considered on loan only, and shall remain the property of His Majesty ...

12.   Any person who:–

(ii) sells or gives to any aboriginal any intoxicating liquor except such as is bona fide administered as a medicine; or

(iii) harbours any aboriginal unless such aboriginal has a certificate or unless a contract of service as aforesaid has been made on his behalf and is then in force, or unless such aboriginal from illness or from the result of any accident or other cause is in urgent need of succour and such cause is reported in writing to the Board or local committee or local guardian or to a justice within one week after the need has arisen; or

(iv) removes or attempts to remove or instigates any other person to remove any aboriginal from Victoria without the written consent in that behalf of the Minister shall be guilty of an offence against this Act ...

From Victoria's Aborigines Act 1915, 6 George V, No. 2610.

QUESTIONS FOR READING 19

How different were the rights of 'protected Aborigines' from those of the general community?

What were Aborigines supposed to be protected from?

Were Aborigines really protected by Acts such as this one?

FURTHER READING

Biskup, P., *Not Slaves, not Citizens: The Aboriginal Problem in Western Australia, 1898–1954*, St Lucia: University of Queensland Press, 1973.

Kidd, R., *The Way We Civilize: Aboriginal Affairs — the Untold Story*, St Lucia: University of Queensland Press, 1997.

Markus, A., *Governing Savages*, Sydney: Allen & Unwin, 1990.

Read, P., *The Stolen Generations: The Removal of Aboriginal Children in New South Wales, 1883 to 1969*, 2nd ed., Sydney: Office of Aboriginal Affairs, 1998.

10   The Assimilation Era, 1937–1960s

It used to be suggested that the 1937 Conference of Commonwealth and State Aboriginal authorities was a great turning point in Aboriginal policy. This is an exaggeration, but there were changes. In the 1920s and 1930s, with improved communications, there was better contact with the outback and more interest in it. This brought home to white city-dwellers the existence of an 'Aboriginal problem'. In the 1920s and 1930s the southern press publicized some notable massacres and cases of injustice in remote areas. These stories stirred consciences as many people in the south became more aware of definite needs and of injustices. For instance, a big enquiry followed the Coniston Massacre in the Northern Territory in 1928 and even many white people believed that the enquiry had been a 'whitewash'.

Meanwhile, the activities of the Christian missions among Aborigines were expanding in scope and number, and the churches were also beginning to apply considerable pressure on governments to adopt a positive policy concerning the Aborigines instead of the negative 'protection-segregation' policy. Ideas of 'mandate' in colonies, coming from the League of Nations, inspired some concern for indigenous races like the Aborigines. From the 1930s anthropology became a university subject; research expanded and more students were exposed to Aboriginal culture. Scholars like A.P. Elkin (Sydney), Donald Thomson (Melbourne) and T.G.H. Strehlow (Adelaide) also

Professor A.P. Elkin (standing, right) on an anthropological expedition at Maranboy, NT, in 1948. On the left is Bill Harney (bush worker and Aboriginal protector) and seated at right, cartoonist Eric Jolliffe (well known for his sympathetic but patronizing 'Witchetty's Tribe' cartoons).

began to speak out, and governments listened. Aboriginal people themselves were stubbornly refusing to die out, and their population even showed signs of increasing. As we have seen, they began to organize for their own benefit in the 1920s and 1930s, notably in Victoria and New South Wales.

Assimilation

Naturally, there were no Aboriginal people at the 1937 conference, nor were they consulted. The result of the conference was a change in aim from passive protection to what was seen as a positive policy described as 'assimilation'. Aborigines not of 'full blood' were to be assimilated within Australian society. (In fact, assimilation of 'half-castes' had already been Victoria's policy since the 1880s and Western Australia's from the 1920s.) As a sign of this change of emphasis, protection boards tended to be renamed 'welfare boards'. In February 1939 the Hon. John McEwen, Minister for the Interior, issued an important statement on Commonwealth policy towards Aborigines. Aborigines were to be educated for full citizenship without distinction either among Aborigines or between them and white people. Progressively, through training and welfare, Aborigines were to be given equal opportunity whenever possible. For the Northern Territory, a Director of Native Affairs (E.W.P. Chinnery) was appointed. The principle that Aboriginal policy ought to be uniform throughout the country was established (though never perfectly achieved). An Australian Council for Native Welfare was set up by federal and state governments to coordinate policies.

Though assimilation was termed 'voluntary' in 1961, the possibility that Aborigines would choose otherwise did not occur to many white people until the 1970s. This was despite recognition by the 1937 conference that something could be learned from the racial situation in America, where Native Americans ('Indians') were already rejecting assimilation.

The states' policies went along much as before, though perhaps more benevolently. At any rate, the effects were not very much different. It might be best to look at some aspects of Commonwealth policy after the McEwen memorandum. Many things remained the same: Aborigines, unsung and under-paid, were the backbone of the Northern Territory's cattle industry. The Second World War interrupted somewhat the thrust of the new assimilation policy. On the other hand, the war years sped social change in the required direction — though in a way accidentally. The important thing was the employment by the Australian Army of many Territory Aborigines as mechanics, construction workers and so on, with relatively high wages, good conditions and adequate food. The frontier had come to an end, and Aborigines now realized what they had lost and what they were missing.

Nevertheless, under a vigorous and idealistic Minister for Territories from 1951 to 1963, Commonwealth policy took important, if faltering, steps forward. This minister was P.M.C. Hasluck and his ideas were old: benevolence, welfare and justice as Governor Gipps had aimed for in 1838. In other ways, he was ahead of his time, and this fact is illustrated by the resistance offered to his basic idea that all Aborigines should be citizens in full standing, with special legislation only applying to exceptions (of any race), rather than vice versa as before.

The Wards Employment Ordinance of 1953 and the Welfare Ordinance of 1959 were the basis of the Northern Territory's 'new policy'. The starting principle was that all Aborigines were citizens but most would need to be educated gradually to exercise all the rights of citizens. During this process, the ordinances applied to people called 'wards', who were actually defined with no mention of race. With a few exceptions, however, all 'full-blooded' Aborigines in the Territory were wards, under the protection, guidance and control of the Native Welfare Department. Those in employment were to be wards-in-training, and not entitled to full wages (like apprentices). To the full-bloods, the policy meant actual denial of citizenship and equal wages, close control of their lives and continued dependence on welfare. Sometimes, full-bloods could be exempted from the effect of the ordinance, thus becoming full citizens, as was the case with painter Albert Namatjira. But this had bad effects, too, when all a man's friends were wards and subject to special laws and he was not, especially as

Minister for Territories, Paul Hasluck, visits the school on Bagot reserve in the Northern Territory in 1958. Later, as Sir Paul Hasluck, he was governor-general.

one of the 'special laws' forbade the use of alcohol. Furthermore, over a half of the Aborigines in the Northern Territory lived on mission or government stations, where supervision and control were easier and, therefore, greater. This control included control of even the residents' meagre wages and social service benefits.

The famous painter Albert Namatjira was freed of the control of being a ward, only to be gaoled in 1958 for supplying alcohol to relatives who were still wards.

The lag between policy and practice may be explained in part as resulting from the inevitable carry-over of personnel to administer the policy. A similar lag affected state policies also. Instead of a triumphant march of Aborigines to equality and citizenship, the main feature of this new deal was bigger, better and more expensive institutional welfare programs. In New South Wales, individuals could be exempted from the Act and be treated as full citizens; they had to carry a card to prove this, which came to be known as the 'dog licence'. One policy which continued from the earlier 'protection era' was the policy of removing allegedly 'at-risk' children from families and their placement in foster families or homes such as Cootamundra and Kinchela in New South Wales and Moore River in Western Australia. This was consistent with the aim of assimilating the Aboriginal population and, as usual, the judgment about whom to remove was made by white authorities and usually carried out by the police. It took no account of the different form of Aboriginal kinship and extended families. Eventually, the 'Stolen Generation' created by this policy would be recognized.

In the remoter areas of the states — north Queensland, most of Western Australia and South Australia — the situation of the Aborigines in the 1950s and 1960s was rather similar. They were being trained

'Deplorable! Something must be done — when we can decide who's to pay for it.'
This cartoon shows Western Australian and federal governments talking about the
problems but doing nothing. (Frith, *Melbourne Herald*, 1957)

The Australian Institute for Aboriginal and Torres Strait Islander Studies (AIATSIS)
was established in Canberra in 1961, to become the world centre for such studies. It
moved to this new building in 2001.

The so-called 'Half-Caste Home' in Darwin, NT, 1928. Even before the official adoption of the aim of 'assimilation' in 1937, therefore, authorities in most states sought to separate such children from 'tribal life' and train them to move into the general community.

Teaching in the Pitjantjatjara language at Ernabella mission in 1958. Policy here had already gone beyond 'assimilation' while it was still official government policy. (Photo by Hamilton Aiken)

rather ineffectively for assimilation, an aim they had not chosen. Those on 'missions' (the word was often loosely used for any government- or church-run reserve or station) even found their movements, money and marriages were controlled. The most thorough and oppressive close supervision was exercised in Queensland but it was only the extent of the control that varied from state to state.

READING 20

The Assimilation Objective Defined in 1937
Commonwealth and state Aboriginal authorities met in Canberra in 1937 and attempted to develop a common national approach to policy towards Aborigines. 'Protection' was rejected in favour of 'assimilation'.

Destiny of the Race
That this Conference believes that the destiny of the natives of aboriginal origin, but not of the full blood, lies in their ultimate absorption by the people of the Commonwealth, and it therefore recommends that all efforts be directed to that end.

Uniformity of Legislation
That the details of administration, in accordance with the general principles agreed upon, be left to the individual States, but there shall be uniformity of legislation as far as possible.

Education and Employment
That, subject to the previous resolution, efforts of all State authorities should be directed towards the education of children of mixed aboriginal blood at white standards, and their subsequent employment under the same conditions as whites with a view to their taking their place in the white community on an equal footing with the whites.

Supervision of Full-Blood Natives
That this Conference affirms the principle that the general policy in respect of full-blood natives should be –

(a)   To educate to white standard, children of the detribalized living near centres of white population, and subsequently to place them in employment in lucrative occupations, which will not bring them into economic or social conflict with the white community.

(b)   To keep the semi-civilized under a benevolent supervision in regard to employment, social and medical service in their own tribal areas. ... The ultimate destiny of these people should be their elevation to class (a).

(c)   To preserve as far as possible the uncivilized native in his normal tribal state by the establishment of inviolable reserves; each State or Territory determining for itself whether mission activities should be conducted on these reserves and the conditions under which they may be permitted.

Aboriginal Welfare: Initial Conference of Commonwealth and State Aboriginal Authorities, Canberra, 1937, p. 3.

QUESTIONS FOR READING 20

How new was this policy?

What choice did Aborigines have in the terms of this policy? (Compare this document with Reading 6, pp. 83–4).

What were the cultural assumptions behind these statements?

FURTHER READING

Griffiths, M., *Aboriginal Affairs: A Short History*, Kenthurst, NSW: Kangaroo Press, 1995.

Kidd, R., *The Way We Civilize: Aboriginal Affairs — the Untold Story*, St Lucia: University of Queensland Press, 1997.

Macleod, C., *Patrol in the Dreamtime*, Melbourne: Mandarin, 1997 (memoirs of a humane ex-patrol officer in the Northern Territory in the 1950s).

Stone, S. (ed.), *Aborigines in White Australia: A Documentary History of Attitudes Affecting Official Policy on the Australian Aborigine, 1697–1973*, Melbourne: Heinemann, 1974.

11 The Rise of Self-Determination, 1967–1990s

In the mid-sixties there began to be signs of some liberalization in Aboriginal policy on the part of state and federal governments. Basically, governments were becoming more ready to consult the Aborigines about desirable policies. On the national level FCAATSI, in particular, began to apply more pressure for greater consultation.

Land Rights

Starting with South Australia with its Aboriginal Lands Trust Act in 1966, most states started to give some sort of land rights to Aborigines. (As early as 1956, South Australia had transferred some land to the Pitjantjatjara people.) Usually, this involved a state-level Lands Trust or regional Lands Councils to control reserves. The New South Wales Aboriginal Lands Trust was set up in 1974 as a body fully elected by Aborigines, with practical autonomy and power over nearly 2840 hectares (7000 acres) of reserve land. There were similar provisions in land rights laws of the other states. In South Australia, Aboriginal land amounted to over 10 per cent of the state's area by 1981. In that year also, the Pitjantjatjara Land Rights Act gave total rights over their traditional land in the north-west of South Australia to this tribe.

Most restrictive or discriminatory legislation (for example, that controlling the use of alcoholic liquor) was repealed, except in

Queensland, where the 1965 Aborigines and Torres Strait Islanders Act actually tightened supervision and control in some respects. Indeed, Queensland was an exception to the overall trend of Aboriginal policies from the mid-sixties.

In 1978, the Queensland state government turned Aurukun and Mornington Island into shires in order to frustrate both the federal government and Uniting Church, which both supported policies of Aboriginal self-management. In 1982, a system of land-holding for Aboriginal communities called 'deeds of grant in trust' was introduced, which fell far short of the kind of land rights accepted elsewhere in Australia. In 1987, freehold title was announced, to a sceptical audience. The Western Australian government had also been dragging its feet with land rights, over the issue of mineral exploration, and while the New South Wales government established a very good system in 1983, by 1986 it had not actually made over as much as .05 per cent of the state's land to Aborigines. In 1985 Uluru (Ayers Rock) was handed back to traditional owners, the Mutitjulu. The South Australian government in 1989 granted land rights to Maralinga, which had been taken for atomic bomb testing in the 1950s.

As was often the case in this field, church mission authorities tended to be in the vanguard of change: residents of many mission stations were given group ownership and control of their land before governments implemented land rights policy in the 1970s. Reserves and missions became communities and missionaries and managers became advisers.

From Integration to Self-Determination
Commonwealth policy, too, began to change. The right to vote was finally granted in 1962; in 1965 the Conciliation and Arbitration Commission approved equal pay for Aborigines; and a 1965 conference modified the aim of government policy from 'assimilation' to voluntary 'integration'. Finally, white Australians gave the seal of approval in the 1967 referendum which removed parts of the Constitution which prevented Aborigines from being counted in the census and prevented

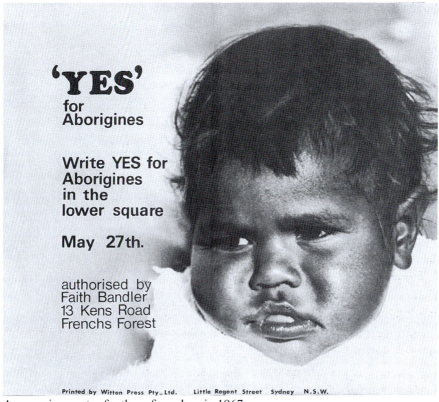

'YES'
for
Aborigines

Write YES for
Aborigines
in the
lower square

May 27th.

authorised by
Faith Bandler
13 Kens Road
Frenchs Forest

Printed by Witton Press Pty., Ltd.   Little Regent Street   Sydney   N.S.W.

A campaign poster for the referendum in 1967.

the Commonwealth parliament from making laws for Aborigines anywhere in Australia. Now, Aboriginal people would be counted in the census and the federal parliament would be allowed to make laws about them. (It is sometimes wrongly assumed that the 1967 referendum gave Aborigines the vote and citizenship.)

It was impressive that over 90 per cent of voters in the referendum voted 'yes', a record level of support in a referendum. Many Aborigines and their supporters felt optimistic about the prospect of reform. The federal Liberal government did indeed make some improvements between 1967 and its defeat in 1972 and actually had a Minister for Aboriginal Affairs for the first time. But it moved slowly; land rights were a sticking point for the government and it was reluctant to

'Referendum 1967.' This cartoon by Bruce Petty in *The Australian* shows the Aboriginal community waiting for preoccupied white voters to vote 'yes' and enable them to move ahead.

override objectionable state laws. (It was largely this disappointment which prompted the famous Tent Embassy, noted in Chapter 7.)

In the 1970s, especially after the Whitlam Labor Government came to power in December 1972, the trend toward greater consultation with Aborigines and more Aboriginal power over their own future accelerated. More Aborigines were administering policy as civil servants. More money was being spent in ways agreed on by Aborigines, generally more often in self-help projects such as housing cooperatives in the city and cattle stations in the outback. In 1974 Aborigines elected a National Aboriginal Consultative Committee to tell Canberra what they wanted. Discrimination — educational, social, legal — was being attacked more and more vigorously.

Under the Fraser Liberal Government's Land Rights Act of 1977,

27 per cent of the Northern Territory became Aboriginal land by 1985. Founded in 1981, the Aboriginal Development Commission provided for self-management on a broad scale, acquiring land and financing commercial ventures and housing. Things were continuing to change in the states also. The New South Wales Aboriginal Land Rights Act of 1983 improved the ability of Aboriginal communities to claim land. In 1987, the Victorian parliament passed Acts to restore land at former missions at Lake Condah and Framlingham to Aboriginal control and to protect Aboriginal heritage. Queensland finally passed an Aboriginal Land Act in 1991

The Freedom Riders of 1965.

Why?

Why was there this great upsurge in interest and action after 1965? Undoubtedly, Aborigines themselves fought for it, as outlined in Chapters 6 and 7. To give two instances: the Gurindji's strike of 1966

Prime Minister Gough Whitlam pours soil into the hand of Vincent Lingiari at Wattie Creek, NT, in 1975, as a symbol of a transfer of land to the Gurindji.

and land rights claim at Wattie Creek in the Northern Territory, and the Yolngu's 'Bark Petition' of 1963 which was followed by their Yirrkala case against the Nabalco mining company 1970–71. Both failed in the short term, but they won changes of attitude in government which meant a greater victory for all Aborigines. Secondly, there was world-wide concern about race problems, in the United States, in South Africa, even in Britain with its Asian and West Indian immigrants; the Australian press and television began to give more publicity to Aboriginal groups and problems and such events as the student Freedom Ride of 1965, led by Charles Perkins, which publicized racial problems in New South Wales country towns.

Australians in general were also becoming more aware of Aborigines through increased Aboriginal immigration into the capital cities, and through the teaching of anthropology, which was far more widely available than even ten years before. Archaeology and anthropology were diffusing more and better information about the Aborigines. Foreign investment in northern Australia also served to bring to public notice areas peopled mainly by Aborigines. Thirdly, the easing of cold war international tension and the increasing acceptance of migrants in the community led to greater openness and tolerance of differences among 'old' white Australians. This made the abandoning of forced assimilation more probable.

Even more significant in the long run was the fact that Aborigines themselves were now implementing as well as helping to shape policy: for instance, Pat O'Shane in 1982 became the first Aboriginal to be the permanent head of a government department, the New South Wales Ministry of Aboriginal Affairs. In 1986, the first Aboriginal cabinet minister was appointed: Western Australia's Minister for Aboriginal Affairs, Ernie Bridge. By 1990, policy-making was increasingly involving Aboriginal people at the highest level.

Policy towards the Aborigines had thus undergone important changes since 1788. From 'friendly relations' to 'civilization' to 'protection' to 'assimilation' to 'integration', the aim changed, with few signs that any aim imposed by Europeans could ever be achieved. Large amounts of money had been wasted. During the 1970s and 1980s, government spending on Aboriginal affairs increased and there was much more Aboriginal influence on how the money was spent. There was still waste, as critics were fond of reporting, but the priorities of spending were at least worked out closer to the needs. For instance, infant mortality was almost halved and overall educational standards rose strongly.

The Beginning of the Search for Reconciliation

After some highly publicized deaths of mainly young male Aboriginal offenders in police cells and gaols, a Royal Commission into Aboriginal Deaths in Custody was set up in 1987 and reported in 1991. It concluded that Aboriginal prisoners were no more likely to die in custody than others but that the real problem was that they were arrested and locked up at a rate many times higher than others. The Commission made 338 recommendations all but one of which were accepted by the federal government.

The bicentenary of European settlement was to be celebrated in 1988. With greater acknowledgement by governments and people of the wrongs done to Aboriginal people in the past, including dispossession of their land, there was a dilemma for governments. How to celebrate what had been largely a tragedy for one segment of the population? On Australia Day, as thousands lined Sydney Harbour to welcome the First Fleet re-enactment, other thousands were demonstrating to say that 'white Australia has a black history'. The activist Burnum Burnum turned the tables by unfurling the Aboriginal flag on Dover beach and claiming England for the Aboriginal nation. The Barunga Statement, demanding national land rights and a treaty, was presented to Prime Minister Bob Hawke, who promised to act. (See Reading 10, pp. 102–03.)This proved legally and politically too difficult.

In 1990, the Aboriginal and Torres Strait Islander Commission (ATSIC) was set up by federal parliament to involve indigenous people in aspects of government affecting them and to oversee several programs and bodies providing services to Aboriginal communities. It was chaired for the first six years by Lowitja (formerly Lois) O'Donoghue from South Australia, who was followed by Northern Territory Yolngu businessman Gatjil Djerrkura from 1996 to 2000. With no legal or political possibility of a treaty, the federal government moved to a concept of a compact of reconciliation and in 1991 established a Council for Aboriginal Reconciliation headed by Evelyn Scott from north Queensland.

Complex issues about how to deal with Aboriginal culture in remote areas concerned politicians and administrators. South Australia passed an Aboriginal Heritage Act. A campaign began in the 1970s to return Aboriginal remains from museums to communities for burial, starting with the skeleton of Truganini being handed back by the Tasmanian Museum in 1976 for cremation. Traditional punishments

Truganini, photographed in 1866, was erroneously seen as the 'last Tasmanian'. Her skeleton was returned to the Aboriginal community in 1976, cremated, and her ashes scattered in the waters of her homeland of Bruny Island.

were sometimes considered in court sentences in remote areas. In 1991, a mine was proposed at Coronation Hill on Jawoyn land in the Kakadu area of the Northern Territory. Debate was centred on interpretations of the religious significance of the hill proposed to be mined, said by some to be the dreaming place of a great lizard.In 1987, there was an unrecognized signal of momentous change to come. In that year, Eddie Mabo and other Torres Strait Islanders commenced legal action against the Queensland government. This case would eventually reach the High Court of Australia, with massive potential for the Torres Strait Islander and Aboriginal campaign for land.

READING 21

Commonwealth Aboriginal Policy in the 1970s
The following extracts are from the platform of the Australian Labor Party, 1973, and reflect changes in thinking on Aboriginal policy in the 1970s.

4.   Educational opportunities to be provided in no way inferior to those of the general community, with special programmes at all levels where

necessary to overcome cultural deprivation and meet special needs. Pre-school education to be provided for every Aboriginal child, including teaching in indigenous languages where desirable. Adult education to be provided as broadly as possible. A programme of technical and managerial training to be developed and the co-operation of the trade union movement to be sought in recognizing Aboriginal skills...

7.   All Aboriginal lands to be vested in a public trust or trusts composed of Aboriginals or Islanders as appropriate. Exclusive corporate land rights to be granted to Aboriginal communities which retain a strong tribal structure or demonstrate a potential for corporate action in regard to land at present reserved for the use of Aboriginals, or where traditional occupancy according to tribal custom can be established from anthropological or other evidence.

No Aboriginal land to be alienated or assigned for any use including mineral development except with the approval both of the Trust and the Parliament. Such Trusts or groups shall be entitled to use capital funds investments to establish community or co-operative ventures for the benefit of local inhabitants. All Aboriginals jointly to share the benefits from the development of natural resources, including minerals, on Aboriginal lands. The sacred sites of the Aboriginals to be mapped and protected...

9.   Every Australian child to be taught the history and culture of Aboriginal and Island Australians as an integral part of the history of Australia.

QUESTIONS FOR READING 21

In what points is the policy outlined here different from previous policies for the Aborigines?

Should Aborigines be taught at school in Aboriginal languages?

Does a government or political party have the right (point 9) to tell teachers what to teach in history?

READING 22

A Proposal for a Treaty

Responding to a decision by the National Aboriginal Conference in 1979, an Aboriginal Treaty Committee of white Australians began campaigning for a Makarrata or Treaty of Commitment between white and black Australians. The chairman was Dr H.C. Coombs.

We the undersigned Australians, of European descent, believe that experience since 1788 has demonstrated the need for the status and rights of Aboriginal Australians and Torres Strait Islanders to be established in a Treaty, Covenant or Convention freely negotiated with the Commonwealth government by their representatives. Australia is the only former British colony not to recognize native title to land. From this first wrong two centuries of injuries have followed. It is time to strike away the past and make a just settlement together.

We believe this would be a signal to the world that Australia acknowledges past injustices and is acting to correct them. Until that signal is given Australia's international reputation as a society based on justice and humanity is threatened …

We urge the Commonwealth Parliament to resolve that the Government should:
(a)   enable the National Aboriginal Conference to summon a convention of representatives nominated by Aboriginal communities and associations to choose negotiators, who would propose the bases of negotiation and the way in which any settlement should be confirmed;
(b)   organize the negotiations;
(c)   submit any Treaty, Covenant or Convention to Parliament for ratification.

We Call for a Treaty Within Australia, Between Australians, leaflet, 1979.

QUESTIONS FOR READING 22

Why did the authors want a treaty?

How was this approach to decision-making different from earlier decision-making in policy towards Aborigines?

FURTHER READING

Griffiths, M., *Aboriginal Affairs, 1967–2005: Seeking a Solution: How and Why We Failed*, Kenthurst, NSW: Rosenberg Publishing, 2006.

Harris, S., *'It's Coming Yet': An Aboriginal Treaty Within Australia Between Australians*, Sydney: Angus & Robertson, 1979.

Partington, Geoffrey, *Hasluck Versus Coombs: White Politics and Australia's Aborigines*, Sydney: Quakers Hill Press, *c.* 1996.

Rowse, T., *Obliged to Be Difficult: Nugget Coombs' Legacy in Indigenous Affairs*, Melbourne: Cambridge University Press, 2000.

12 Mabo, Wik and Reconciliation

Though not successful in the past, Aboriginal people continued to pursue their rights in the courts. In 1987 a Torres Strait Islander living in Townsville, Eddie Mabo, and some of his friends began legal action against the Queensland government in order to assert his rights over his land on Mer, or the Murray Islands of the Torres Strait. Eventually, the case found its way to the High Court in Canberra on appeal. In 1992, the High Court gave its decision in Mabo v. Queensland, recognizing the existence of pre-existing 'native title' to land, specifically to the Murray Islands but potentially opening the way for recognition of Native Title rights across Australia. The decision also rejected the previous assumption that Australia was a waste-land which did not actually belong to anyone before 1788. (The 1970s term *terra nullius* was used later to describe this.) Until 1992, this had been the legal basis for determining land tenure in Australia. The Chief Justice wrote that Native Title was the 'interests and rights of Indigenous inhabitants in land, whether communal, group or individual, possessed under the traditional laws acknowledged and the traditional customs observed by the Indigenous inhabitants'. The court found that this right continued in Torres Strait and might, in principle, be found to apply to some parts of the mainland of Australia.

Eddie Mabo (left), pictured on Mer (Murray Island) in Torres Strait.

In late 1992, Labor Prime Minister Paul Keating had given his Redfern speech to launch United Nations Year for Indigenous People in 1993, frankly admitting the evils of the past. In 1993 federal parliament passed the Native Title Act, the federal government's response to the Mabo decision. The Act set up an Indigenous Land Fund and the Native Title Tribunal, which was designed to provide an alternative to having to go through lengthy and expensive legal process for each Native Title claim as the Murray Islanders had had to do. Next, the Wik people of far northern Queensland took their claim that native title could co-exist with pastoral leases to the High Court, which in 1996 brought down the Wik judgement. This judgement agreed with their claim but stated that where there was any conflict of use, the rights of the pastoralist would prevail.

It was not all easy going for Aboriginal policy in the 1990s and 2000s. There was something of a backlash against land rights, the 'Aboriginal industry' and 'special treatment' for Aborigines, partly associated with an independent member elected to federal parliament in 1996, Pauline Hanson. The consensus between political parties in parliament over Aboriginal issues was upset somewhat but services to Aboriginal communities were not reduced. There were, however, to be changes in the way that government services were delivered. Allegations of corruption and inefficiency in ATSIC also contributed to this change of mood.

When it came to making Native Title claims, it proved to be difficult for Aboriginal communities in the settled parts of the country to prove that native title continued. One huge claim, by the Yorta Yorta of the Murray Valley, was rejected after a struggle from 1994 to 2003. A Federal Court judge wrote that 'the tide of history has indeed washed away any real acknowledgement of their traditional laws and any real observance of their traditional customs'. Nevertheless, in 2004, the Victorian state government reached an agreement with the Yorta Yorta that acknowledged their land management rights through co-management of 50,000 hectares of Crown land. On the other hand, the Dhangadi on the north coast of New South Wales made the first successful claim in that state in 1997. Court cases in 2001 and 2004 established that that native title rights co-exist in the sea. By 2004, however, only 50 native title claims had been successful. In Western Australia in 2006, the Federal Court recognized the Native Title of the Noongar people of the Perth area. In 2007, the Githabul and the New South Wales state government signed the biggest ever native title deal in that state. An Indigenous Land Use Agreement covers 6000 square kilometres in the north-east of the state near Mount Lindesay, where the Githabul gained joint managerial control of national parks and control over future development on the land.

Practical Reconciliation?
In 1996 a Liberal government led by Prime Minister John Howard was elected and was almost immediately confronted with the Wik judgement. In the meantime, the new government was seeking to distance itself (not very successfully) from claims by the expelled party member but independent MP, Pauline Hansen, that there was government discrimination in favour of Aborigines and that they were given benefits unavailable to white Australians.

In responding to the Wik judgement, the government developed a Ten-Point Plan, which tried to find a compromise to keep miners, graziers and Aborigines happy. In the event, no one was happy. *Bringing Them Home*, the report by the Human Rights and Equal Opportunities Commission on the Stolen Generations, was released in 1997 by its chairman, Sir Ronald Wilson. At the Reconciliation

Cartoon before the 1998 federal election, just after the Wik case decision. (Prior, *Canberra Times*)

conference held that year, the prime minister was booed. A political campaign followed to force the prime minister to say 'sorry'. This he persistently refused to do, arguing that the present generation was not responsible for the evils of the past, that it would make no practical difference to Aboriginal disadvantage and that the sovereign body was the parliament and in 1999 it had passed a resolution of reconciliation which expressed 'its deep and sincere regret'. (See Reading 23.)

Ordinary citizens organized annual 'sorry days' and members of a band at the closing ceremony of the Sydney Olympics in 2000 wore 'sorry' T-shirts. Australians for Native Title and Reconciliation (ANTaR) organized activities to highlight the issue, such as the concept of a multi-coloured 'sea of hands'. In 2005, the National Sorry Day Committee renamed Sorry Day as a National Day of Healing for all Australians.

Despite the emphasis of the new government on 'practical' solutions, symbolic issues remained important to many people.

Between 1995 and 1998, the building of the Hindmarsh Island Bridge near the mouth of the Murray River was temporarily halted because it might interfere with Aboriginal 'secret women's business'. There was conflict in the general community because the nature of the 'secret women's business' could not be tested and this increased when some senior Ngarrindjeri women claimed that the 'secret women's business' was a fabrication. There were a Royal Commission, court cases and an Act of federal parliament before the bridge was finally allowed to be built.

Doreen Kartinyeri, scholar of the Ngarrindjerri people of South Australia. Her research was the basis of claims of 'secret women's business' affecting Hindmarsh Island.

In the 1990s, a struggle broke out over Australia's history, especially over whether Australians ought to be ashamed or proud of their past or, to put it another way, whether Australians should wear a 'black armband' or a 'white blindfold'. This became known as the history wars. The major focus was race relations, especially between black and white. The issue was brought to the fore by the work of historian Keith Windschuttle, who questioned the extent of violent Aboriginal deaths on the frontier and the methods and motives of some historians in his *The Fabrication of Aboriginal History* (2002). There was much focus on particular massacres and whether they really happened, or had been exaggerated, and also on the intent of governments and settlers in clashes. The use of the term *terra nullius* was also questioned. On both sides, the debate became political and personal and therefore tended to avoid coming to grips with valid criticisms, to obscure the importance of the subject matter and generate more heat than light. In the long run, it should also encourage more, and more careful, research. It has already made many white and black people more aware of the importance of knowing how their history has been written.

The idea of 'mainstreaming' government services was a part of 'practical reconciliation', whereby services for Aborigines would be provided by the same agencies that provided them for all citizens. There would be help for those in need but not on a racial basis. In 2005, ATSIC was formally abolished and its functions distributed amongst various federal agencies. In 2003, an experiment began with a 'whole-of-government' approach in eight separate communities. The aim was to get all levels of government to work together in ways sensitive to local conditions. There were some disagreements within the communities and some public servants failed to understand local cultures. In Balgo, Western Australia, crime rates were reduced but the trial in Shepparton, Victoria, which aimed to develop education and jobs was reported to be less successful. From 2006, the policy and coordination role of the federal government was the responsibility of the Office of Indigenous Policy Coordination in the Department of Families, Community Services and Indigenous Affairs. In place of ATSIC, the National Indigenous Council was established as the main source of advice to the federal government on indigenous matters but it was appointed by government, not elected.

That a change of approach was required was underlined by increasing criticism of waste, corruption and inefficiency of many Aboriginal agencies responsible for services from indigenous leaders themselves. (See Reading 11, pp. 104–05.) One example of such self-criticism was the 2006 Summit meeting to discuss serious alcohol, drug and violence problems in remote communities. Education, health, employment, substance abuse, child abuse and domestic violence thus continued to be very serious issues for many Aboriginal communities.

Dramatic intervention by the federal government in Northern Territory communities after a damning report on sexual abuse of children in 2007 produced contradictory responses. Some Aboriginal leaders like Noel Pearson and Marcia Langton guardedly welcomed the initiative; more of the older leaders condemned it as heavy-handed, discriminatory and paternalistic. Were the problems so severe that normal legal and constitutional rights needed to be set aside?

The results of a riot at Palm Island community, north Queensland, in 2004. A police officer was alleged to have caused the death of an Aboriginal prisoner.

Noel Pearson, a law graduate and a leader in Aboriginal affairs since the 1990s, is pictured here as director of the Cape York Institute for Policy and Leadership. He has been critical of welfare dependence.

The change of federal government in 2007 was hailed by many indigenous and non-indigenous Australians as an opportunity for a fresh start, with the Kevin Rudd-led Labor Party government promising to make an apology to the 'Stolen Generation', a promise fulfilled on the second day of sitting of the new parliament, on 13 February 2008. (See Reading 24, pp. 171–72.) The new government modified but nevertheless continued the special intervention into Northern Territory communities which had been initiated by its predecessor. It remains to be seen whether the will to solve these problems can overcome political interests and factions within and outside Aboriginal communities, and involve Aboriginal leaders and citizens, administrators and parliaments working together.

READING 23

Federal Parliament's Resolution of Reconciliation in 1999

[The House of Representatives resolved that it:]

(a) reaffirms its wholehearted commitment to the cause of reconciliation between Indigenous and non-indigenous Australians as an important national priority for Australians;

(b) recognizing the achievements of the Australian nation, commits to work together to strengthen the bonds that unite us, to respect and appreciate our differences and to build a fair and prosperous future in which we can all share;

(c) reaffirms the central importance of practical measures leading to practical results that address the profound economic and social disadvantage which continues to be experienced by many indigenous Australians;

(d) recognizes the importance of understanding the shared history of indigenous and non-indigenous Australians and the need to acknowledge openly the wrongs and injustices of Australia's past;

(e) acknowledges that the mistreatment of many indigenous Australians over a significant period represents the most blemished chapter in our national history;

(f) expresses its deep and sincere regret that indigenous Australians suffered injustices under the practices of past generations, and for the hurt and trauma that many indigenous people continue to feel as a consequence of those practices; and

(g) believes that we, having achieved so much as a nation, can now move forward together for the benefit of all Australians.

Hansard, House of Representatives, 26 August 1999.

QUESTIONS FOR READING 23

Do you think this resolution constituted an apology?

Is the wording of section (e) the same as saying 'sorry'? What might be lacking?

How are the words of this motion related to policies adopted by governments and reconciliation activities undertaken by Aboriginal and non-Aboriginal Australians between 1999 and 2007?

READING 24

The Apology Issued by Prime Minister Kevin Rudd in February 2008

Today we honour the Indigenous peoples of this land, the oldest continuing cultures in human history.

We reflect on their past mistreatment.

We reflect in particular on the mistreatment of those who were Stolen Generations — this blemished chapter in our nation's history.

The time has now come for the nation to turn a new page in Australia's history by righting the wrongs of the past and so moving forward with confidence to the future.

We apologize for the laws and policies of successive Parliaments and governments that have inflicted profound grief, suffering and loss on these our fellow Australians.

We apologize especially for the removal of Aboriginal and Torres Strait Islander children from their families, their communities and their country.

For the pain, suffering and hurt of these stolen generations, their descendants and for their families left behind, we say sorry.

To the mothers and the fathers, the brothers and the sisters, for the breaking up of families and communities, we say sorry.

And for the indignity and degradation thus inflicted on a proud people and a proud culture, we say sorry.

We the Parliament of Australia respectfully request that this apology be received in the spirit in which it is offered as part of the healing of the nation.

Hansard, House of Representatives, 13 February 2008.

QUESTION FOR READING 24

Compare this speech with resolution in Reading 23. What difference did the use of the word 'sorry' make?

FURTHER READING

Attwood, B. (ed.), *In the Age of Mabo*, Sydney: Allen & Unwin, 1994.

Griffiths, M., *Aboriginal Affairs, 1967–2005: Seeking a Solution: How and Why We Failed*, Kenthurst, NSW: Rosenberg Publishing, 2006.

13   Conclusion

'Being Australian' is a slippery concept. In *The Chant of Jimmie Blacksmith*, Australian novelist Thomas Keneally painted a powerful picture of a 'half-caste' Aboriginal in 1900, caught between two worlds, rejecting one and being rejected by the other. The story is set in the period when the six Australian colonies were about to become a nation. There is a glaring contrast between white celebrations of nation on the one hand and white neglect and oppression of the original Australians on the other. The novel is based on the true story of Jimmy Governor, a story which illustrates well some of the dilemmas of race in Australia and is, therefore, worth looking at in more detail.

Jimmy Governor was a fairly well-educated and well-behaved 'mission black', who was conscious of being as good as white men. But because he was half-Aboriginal he was tagged as a 'black' and could not, therefore, obtain as good as a job as he was capable of doing. By becoming a New South Wales police tracker in 1896 he virtually accepted that he was a black man. He

Jimmy Governor.

could not own land, though he had worked acceptably as a contract labourer for many settlers.

In the climate of opinion of the day, Governor made a bad mistake in December 1898 when he married a white girl, Ethel Page. Apart from his colour, Governor was a more than eligible match for the girl: he was better educated, a good worker, honest, handsome, a non-drinker and an excellent horseman. But, to the white community, Jimmy Governor was an 'uppity black', trying to rise above his rightful place. Meanwhile, Jimmy had also given up tracking and resumed contract work around Gulgong so he could earn his own independent living. He wanted to be a free person, not a 'black'. It was the marriage which caused the most trouble; racial and sexual feelings were a powerful combination. White men were angry that an Aboriginal had actually married a white girl; white women regarded Ethel as a tramp for marrying an Aboriginal. Probably both fear and jealousy were mixed with these feelings.

The benevolent policy of protection was in its heyday in 1900, but its practical uselessness was obvious to most and encouraged by some whites. Jimmy and Ethel had a church wedding. Indeed, much of Jimmy's dignity was related to a sense of self-worth acquired through mission training, and what little kindness and sympathy he later received came from church quarters. Again, this sympathy was ineffectual in a racist community. Though Jimmy Governor tried, he could not (and perhaps did not really want to) cast off his Aboriginal background. He could hunt and track and could not rid himself of 'freeloading' relatives.

In January 1900, Jimmy, Ethel and baby Sidney Governor moved 80 miles away to Breelong (near Gilgandra) in an attempt to escape from old associations and become independent and accepted in the white community. Unfortunately, the old problems arose. The pay was barely enough for keep no matter how hard Jimmy worked, and his wife was treated with contempt by the white women. Annoyance and frustration grew, despite superficial good relations. The arrival of black friends and relations only made things worse for Jimmy, as he had more mouths to feed on his very low wage. His employer was stingy once too often and his employer's wife uttered one too many insults. On 20 July 1900, Jimmy Governor went berserk. Possibly something like this crossed his mind: if they call me a savage and treat me like one despite all my efforts to be a good citizen, then I might as well act like a savage. With help from a full-blood called Jacky Underwood, he killed or mortally wounded five women and children in the employer's homestead. Jimmy, his brother Joe, and Jacky Underwood led the police an epic chase before Joe was shot and Jimmy and Jacky were captured, tried, convicted and hanged.

It took something like a mass murder and dramatic manhunt to remind the majority of whites, who never saw an Aboriginal in their comfortable cities, of the existence of Aborigines. Indifference, embarrassment, fear, hate and bumbling benevolence were the confused reactions of the white public. They were at this time celebrating the inauguration of a nation which had no place for the Aborigines, except at best a comfortable corner in which to die out. Few paused to consider what sort of society could turn an honest, hard-working, teetotal family man into a mass murderer. Rather, they wondered what they had done to deserve Jimmy — after all, blankets were given out annually, and missionaries and policemen did what they could. As long as white people thought of Aborigines (if they thought of them at all) as blacks and not as people, and treated them accordingly, this lack of understanding would remain.

Significantly, the Governors were always referred to as blacks, never as half-European. Obviously, the 'black half' had to be responsible for Jimmy's crimes. In fact, of course, in the 112 years before Jimmy's 'revenge', far more Aborigines had been killed by whites than vice versa. Very few Aborigines had been convicted of murder in the past, but the Governor brothers caused far more terror in the white community than 'ordinary' murderers. Perhaps the reason for this was guilty white consciences. If they had realized that Jimmy hero-worshipped Ned Kelly, they might have had cause to ponder more deeply what Jimmy represented and what it all meant.

In October 2008, several youths of Pacific Islander background allegedly bashed and killed an Aboriginal man in a outer suburban Brisbane park, just before his famous nephew was due to play for Australia in a rugby league match. Outside the courtroom later, grieving relatives of the dead man were heard to complain, among other things, that immigrants seemed to be unwilling to assimilate to Australian ways. Notwithstanding some inherent irony here, these sentiments underline the changeability and complexity of identity and culture along with the constancy of human nature, 108 years after Jimmy Governor.

Much has changed since 1900, but some things — especially attitudes in country towns — have been slower to improve and in some areas there is a fear that conditions have worsened. After about 180 years of settlement, however, Aboriginal communities were increasingly able to assert themselves and to lay claim to lost dignity and rights. Indigenous people were individually and collectively determined to make their own decisions, to define their own identities, to express their cultures and values in their own ways, to decide their own futures. While the story of the last 40 years or so is a mixed one, governments can no longer simply tell the Indigenous people what is good for them. By 2009, they were better able to decide their own futures than ever before.

FURTHER READING

On the Jimmy Governor case, see:
Clune, F., *Jimmy Governor*, Sydney: Horwitz, 1970.
Davies, B., *The Life of Jimmy Governor*, Sydney: Ure Smith, 1979.
Keneally, T., *The Chant of Jimmie Blacksmith*, Melbourne: Penguin, 1973.
Reynolds, H., 'Jimmy Governor and Jimmie Blacksmith', *Australian Literary Studies*, May 1979, pp. 14–25.

Some other biographies of Aboriginal people:

Clark, M.T., *Pastor Doug*, Melbourne: Lansdowne, 1956.

Horner, J., *Vote Ferguson for Aboriginal Freedom: A Biography*, 2nd ed., Canberra: J. Horner, 1994.

Miller, J., *Koori: A Will to Win*, Sydney: Angus & Robertson, 1985.

O'Donoghue, L., *Lowitja*, Kingswood, SA: Working Title Press, 2003.

Pepper, P., *You Are What You Make Yourself to Be: The Story of a Victorian Aboriginal Family*, Melbourne: Hyland House, 1989.

Purcell, L., *Black Chicks Talking*, Sydney: Hodder Headline, 2002.

Shaw, B., and G. Ngabidj, *My Country of the Pelican Dreaming*, Canberra: AIAS, 1981.

For something different:

McLaren, Jack, *My Crowded Solitude*, Melbourne: Sun, 1966 (a sensitive account by a white man of living with tribal Aborigines on Cape York in 1911).

The Aboriginal Children's History of Australia, Melbourne: Rigby, 1977.

Additional References

These references are additional to the lists after each chapter.

GENERAL REFERENCES

Arthur, W., and F. Morphy (eds), *Macquarie Atlas of Indigenous Australia: Culture and Society Through Space and Time*, Sydney: Macquarie Library, 2005.

Horton, D. (ed.), *The Encyclopaedia of Aboriginal Australia: Aboriginal and Torres Strait Islander History, Society and Culture*, 2 vols, Canberra: Aboriginal Studies Press for the Australian Institute of Aboriginal and Torres Strait Islander Studies, 1994.

ABORIGINAL CULTURE

Berndt, R.M., and C.H. Berndt (eds), *The World of the First Australians*, 3rd ed., Sydney: Lansdowne, 1981.

Bourke, C., E. Bourke and W.H. Edwards (eds), *Aboriginal Australia: An Introductory Reader in Aboriginal Studies*, 2nd ed., Brisbane: University of Queensland Press, 1998.

Edwards, W.H. (ed.), *Traditional Aboriginal Society*, 2nd ed., South Melbourne: Macmillan, 1998.

Robinson, R. (ed.), *Aboriginal Myths and Legends*, Melbourne: Sun, 1966.

Journals: *Oceania*, *Mankind* and *Australian Aboriginal Studies*.

ABORIGINAL PREHISTORY

Isaacs, J. (ed.), *Australian Dreaming: 40,000 Years of Aboriginal History*, Sydney: Lansdowne, 1980.

Lourandos, H., *Continent of Hunter-Gatherers: New Perspectives in Australian Prehistory*, Cambridge: Cambridge University Press, 1997.

Mulvaney, D.J., and J. Kamminga, *The Prehistory of Australia*, 3rd ed., Sydney: Allen & Unwin, 1999.

Mulvaney, D.J., and J.P. White (eds), *Australians to 1788*, Sydney: Fairfax, Syme & Weldon, 1987.

Murray, T. (ed.), *Archaeology of Aboriginal Australia: A Reader*, Sydney: Allen & Unwin, 1998.

Presland, G., *Aboriginal Melbourne: The Lost Land of the Kulin People*, Melbourne: Penguin, 1998.

ABORIGINAL–EUROPEAN RELATIONS

Attwood, B., and S.G. Foster, *Frontier Conflict: The Australian Experience*, Canberra: National Museum of Australia, 2003.

Broome, R., 'The Struggle for Australia: Aboriginal–European Warfare, 1770–1930', in M. McKernan and M. Browne (eds), *Australia: Two Centuries of War and Peace*, Canberra: Australian War Memorial/Sydney: Allen & Unwin, 1988, pp. 92–120.

Broome, R., *Aboriginal Victorians: A History Since 1800*, Sydney: Allen & Unwin, 2005.

Chapman, V., and P. Read (eds), *Terrible Hard Biscuits: A Reader in Aboriginal History*, Sydney: Allen & Unwin / Aboriginal History, 1996.

Connor, J., *The Australian Frontier Wars, 1788–1838*, Sydney: University of New South Wales Press, 2002.

Corris, P.R., *Aborigines and Europeans in Western Victoria*, Canberra: Australian Institute of Aboriginal Studies, 1968.

Critchett, J., *A Distant Field of Murder: Western District Frontiers, 1834–1848*, Melbourne: Melbourne University Press, 1992.

Elkin, A.P., 'Reaction and Interaction: A Food Gathering People and European Settlement in Australia', *American Anthropologist*, Vol. 53, 1951, pp. 164–86. Reprinted in P. Bohannan and F. Plog (eds), *Beyond the Frontier*, Garden City, NY: Natural History Press, 1967, pp. 43–70.

Jenkin, G., *Conquest of the Ngarrindjeri*, Adelaide: Rigby, 1979.

Loos, N.A., *Invasion and Resistance: Aboriginal–European Relations on the Northern Queensland Frontier, 1861–1897*, Canberra: Australian National University Press, 1982.

Mulvaney, D.J., *Encounters in Place: Outsiders and Aboriginal Australians,*

1606–1985, Brisbane: University of Queensland Press, 1989.

Perkins, R. (ed.), *First Australians: An Illustrated History*, Melbourne: Melbourne University Press, 2008.

Rintoul, S., *The Wailing: A National Black Oral History*, Melbourne: William Heinemann, 1993.

Ryan, L., *The Aboriginal Tasmanians*, 2nd ed., Sydney: Allen & Unwin, 1996.

Stevens, F.S. (ed.), *Racism: The Australian Experience, Vol. 2: Black Versus White*, Sydney: Australia and New Zealand Book Company, 1972.

Willey, K., *When the Sky Fell Down: The Destruction of the Tribes of the Sydney Region*, Sydney: Collins, 1979.

Windschuttle, K., *The Fabrication of Aboriginal History, Vol. 1: Van Diemen's Land, 1803–1847*, Sydney: Macleay Press, 2003.

Journal: *Aboriginal History*.

GOVERNMENT POLICY AND ABORIGINES

Coombs, H.C., *Kulinma: Listening to Aboriginal Australians*, Canberra: Australian National University Press, 1978.

Doukakis, A., *The Aboriginal People, Parliament and 'Protection' in New South Wales, 1856–1916*, Sydney: Federation Press, 2006.

Reynolds, H., *Frontier: Aborigines, Settlers and Land*, Sydney: Allen & Unwin, 1987.

Rowley, C.D., *A Matter of Justice*, Canberra: Australian National University Press, 1978.

WHITE ATTITUDES TO ABORIGINES

Dutton, G., *White on Black: The Australian Aborigine Portrayed in Art*, Melbourne: Macmillan, 1974.

Goot, M., and T. Rowse, *Divided Nation? Indigenous Affairs and the Imagined Public,* Melbourne: Melbourne University Press, 2007.

Healy, C., *Forgetting Aborigines*, Sydney: UNSW Press, 2008.

Healy, J.J., *Literature and the Aborigine in Australia, 1770–1975*, Brisbane: University of Queensland Press, 1978.

Macintyre, S., and S. Janson (eds), *Through White Eyes*, Sydney: Allen & Unwin/Australian Historical Studies, 1990.

Mulvaney, D.J., 'The Australian Aborigines, 1606–1929: Opinion and Fieldwork', Parts 1 and 2, in J.J. Eastwood and F.B. Smith (eds), *Historical Studies: Selected Articles, First Series*, Melbourne: Melbourne University Press, 1964 and 1967, pp. 1–56.

Reynolds, H., 'Racial Thought in Early Colonial Australia', *Australian Journal of Politics and History*, April 1974, pp. 45–53.

Stanner, W.E.H., *White Man Got no Dreaming: Essays, 1938–1973*, Canberra: Australian National University Press, 1979.

Wright, J., *We Call for a Treaty*, Sydney: Collins, 1985.

THE ABORIGINAL RIGHTS MOVEMENT

Curthoys, A., *Freedom Ride: A Freedom Rider Remembers*, Sydney: Allen & Unwin, 2002.

Goodall, H., *Invasion to Embassy: Land in Aboriginal Politics in New South Wales, 1770–1972*, Sydney: Allen & Unwin, 1996.

Markus, A. (ed.), *Blood From a Stone: William Cooper and the Australian Aborigines' League*, Melbourne: Monash Publications in History, 1986.

Ramsland J., and C. Mooney, *Remembering Aboriginal Heroes: Struggle, Identity and the Media*, Melbourne: Brolga Publishing, 2007.

Sutton, P., *Native Title and the Descent of Rights*, Perth: National Native Title Tribunal, 1998.

Taffe, S., *Black and White Together: FCAATSI: The Federal Council for the Advancement of Aborigines and Torres Strait Islanders, 1958–1973*, Brisbane: University of Queensland Press, 2005.

BIOGRAPHIES

Attwood, B., and A. Markus, *Thinking Black: William Cooper and Australian Aborigines' League*, Canberra: Australian Institute of Aboriginal and Torres Strait Islander Studies, 2004.

Burger, A., *Neville Bonner: A Biography*, Melbourne: Macmillan, 1979.

Ellis, V.R., *Trucanini: Queen or Traitor?*, Canberra: AIAS, 1981.

Flick, I., and H. Goodall, *Isabel Flick: The Many Lives of an Extraordinary Aboriginal Woman*, Sydney: Allen & Unwin, 2004.

Goolagong, E., and B. Collins, *Evonne*, London: Hart-Davis MacGibbon, 1975.

Gordon, H., *The Embarrassing Australian*, Melbourne: Lansdowne, 1962 (about Reg Saunders, the first Aboriginal army officer).

Graham, T., *Mabo: Life of an Island Man*, Currency Press, Sydney, 1999.

Hall, R.A., *Fighters From the Fringe: Aborigines and Torres Strait Islanders Recall the Second World War*, Canberra: Aboriginal Studies Press, 1995.

Holmes, S.L., *Yirawala — Artist and Man*, Brisbane: Jacaranda, 1972.

Lamilami, L., *Lamilami Speaks*, Sydney: Ure Smith, 1974.

Langford Ginibi, R., *Real Deadly*, Sydney: Angus & Robertson, 1992.

Matthews, J., *The Two Worlds of Jimmie Barker: The Life of an Australian Aboriginal, 1900–1972*, Canberra: AIAS, 1977.

Read, P., *Charles Perkins: A Biography*, rev. ed., Melbourne: Penguin, 2001.

Rose, L., *Lionel Rose — Australian*, Sydney: Angus & Robertson, 1969.

Roughsey, Dick, *Moon and Rainbow*, Sydney: Reed, 1972.

Roughsey, E., *An Aboriginal Mother Tells of the Old and the New*, Melbourne: McPhee Gribble/Penguin, 1984 (about the Lardil people of Mornington Island).

Shaw, B., *Our Heart is the Land: Aboriginal Reminiscences from the Western Lake Eyre Basin*, Canberra: Aboriginal Studies Press, 1995.

Thaiday, W., *Under the Act*, Townsville: Black Publishing, 1981.

Willmot, E., *Pemulwuy the Rainbow Warrior*, Sydney: Weldon, 1987.

WOMEN

Bell, D., *Daughters of the Dreaming*, 3rd ed., Melbourne: Spinifex, 1983.

Gale, F. (ed.), *We Are Bosses Ourselves*, Canberra: AIAS, 1983.

Gale, F. (ed.), *Woman's Role in Aboriginal Society*, 3rd ed., Canberra: AIAS, 1978.

Maris, H., and S. Borg, *Women of the Sun*, Melbourne: Penguin, 1985.

Purcell, L., *Black Chicks Talking*, Sydney: Hodder Headline, 2002.

Simon, E., *Through My Eyes*, Adelaide: Rigby, 1978.

White, I. *et al.* (eds), *Fighters and Singers: The Lives of Some Aboriginal Women*, Sydney: Allen & Unwin, 1985.

BIBLIOGRAPHIES

Hill, M., and A. Barlow, *Black Australia 2: An Annotated Bibliography and Teacher's Guide to Resources on Aborigines and Torres Strait Islanders*, Canberra: AIAS, 1985.

See Websites below, p. 184.

MISCELLANEOUS

Butlin, N.G., *Our Original Aggression: Aboriginal Populations of Southeastern Australia, 1788–1850*, Sydney: Allen & Unwin, 1983.

Davis, J. *et al.* (eds), *Paperbark: A Collection of Black Australian Writings.* Brisbane: University of Queensland Press, 1990.

Duguid, C., *No Dying Race*, Adelaide: Rigby, 1963, 1978.

Harris, J.W., *One Blood: 200 Years of Aboriginal Encounter with Christianity: A Story of Hope*, Sydney: Albatross, 1990, rev. ed., 1994.

Hercus, L., and P. Sutton, *This Is What Happened: Historical Narratives by Aborigines*, Canberra: AIAS, 1986.

Maynard, J., *Aboriginal Stars of the Turf: Jockeys of Australian Racing History*, Canberra: Aboriginal Studies Press, 2003.

Mulvaney, D.J., *Cricket Walkabout: The Australian Aboriginal Cricketers on Tour, 1867–68*, Melbourne: Melbourne University Press, 1967.

Shoemaker, A., *Black Words White Page: Aboriginal Literature, 1929–1988*, St Lucia: University of Queensland Press, 1989.

Taylor, P., *Telling it Like it Is: A Guide to Making Aboriginal and Torres Strait Islander History*, Canberra: AIATSIS, 1992.

Websites

Aboriginal Studies WWW Virtual Library: The Internet Guide to Aboriginal Studies
http://www.ciolek.com/WWWVL-Aboriginal.html
Headings for this comprehensive portal site are: General Resources, Indigenous News Online (ABC, Australia), Koori Web Resources, University Programs, Governmental Web Resources, Aboriginal History, Intercultural Relationships, Australian Native Title, Aboriginal Languages, Aboriginal Art & Culture, Aboriginal Studies Bibliographies, Aboriginal Online Bookstore, Australian Aboriginal Art web sites worldwide.

Australian Institute of Aboriginal and Torres Strait Islander Studies, based in Canberra.
http://www.aiatsis.gov.au/
Research centre, publisher, has the greatest archival collection in the field. Comprehensive online catalogue.

NSW Higher School Certificate online: Aboriginal Studies
http://hsc.csu.edu.au/ab_studies/

Aboriginal Studies Webquest
http://www.teachers.ash.org.au/wattle/abstuds/index.htm

Barani: Indigenous History of Sydney City
http://www.cityofsydney.nsw.gov.au/barani/
An interactive, searchable resource, including a thematic introduction to Sydney's Indigenous history with links to biographies, useful contacts, and references to books, films, images and websites

Mission Voices
An ABC site on Victorian Koori life.
http://www.abc.net.au/missionvoices/default.htm

Mabo — The Native Title Revolution
(See also Audio-visual list, below)
http://www.mabonativetitle.com/

Audio Visual Material

Note: Videos and DVDs are often available for hire from state film libraries, the National Library of Australia and/or school and university libraries.

SOME FEATURE FILMS WITH ABORIGINAL THEMES

Jedda	1955, director: Charles Chauvel
Walkabout	1971, Nicholas Roeg
Badlands	1977, Phillip Noyce
The Last Wave	1977, Peter Weir
The Chant of Jimmie Blacksmith	1978, Fred Schepisi
We of the Never Never	1982, Igor Auzins
The Fringe Dwellers	1986, Bruce Beresford
Bedevil	1993, Tracey Moffatt
Radiance	1998, Rachel Perkins
Yolngu Boy	2001, Stephen Johnson
One Night the Moon	2001, Rachel Perkins
The Tracker	2002, Rolf de Heer
Australian Rules	2002, Paul Goldman
Beneath Clouds	2002, Ivan Sen
Black and White	2002, Craig Lahiff
Rabbit-Proof Fence	2002, Phillip Noyce
Ten Canoes	2006, Rolf de Heer and Peter Djigirr
Australia	2008, Baz Luhrmann

PREHISTORY AND TRADIONAL CULTURE

A Walbiri Fire Ceremony: Ngatjakula (1977, 21 mins, available on DVD from AIATSIS). Ngatjakula is a ceremony of the Walbiri people of Central Australia in which fire is used to punish transgressors of the law.

Back Trackers: Aboriginal and Torres Strait Islander People Making History (1992, 24 mins, available on DVD from AIATSIS). This was commissioned by AIATSIS in association with the Department of Employment, Education and Training as part of the National Reconciliation and Schooling Strategy.

Desert People (1966, 49 mins, available as DVD from Film Australia). A day in the life of two nomadic families of the Australian Western Desert, excerpted from *People of the Australian Western Desert* (a five-hour black-and-white film produced in 1965 and 1967).

Gulpilil — One Red Blood (2007, DVD, 80 mins, available from Ronin Films). A documentary which traces the twin lives of David Gulpilil — an actor appearing in films from *Walkabout* to *Ten Canoes*; and a traditional member and elder of an Aboriginal community in the Northern Territory.

Lalai Dreamtime: Floating This Time (1975, DVD, colour, 55 mins). Concerns the passing on of traditional lore.

Becoming Aboriginal (1978, film, colour, 11 mins, DVD Film Australia). Concerns growing up at Bamyili, NT and explains the education of Aboriginal children in schools and in their communities.

At the Canoe Camp (1980, colour, 39 mins, DVD Film Australia). About daily life near Yirrkala, NT.

POST-CONTACT HISTORY

Babakiueria (1986, DVD, colour, 30 mins, ABC-TV). A light-hearted satire that reverses the roles, imagining what it would be like if a black fleet arrived to settle an area inhabited by white natives and proceeded to control their lives.

Black Magic (1988, DVD, colour, 55 mins, available from Ronin Films). About how Noongars in Western Australia used sport to seek social advancement.

Frontier (1996, ABC series, three episodes of 60 mins each, DVD). The story of race relations on the frontier, based on the books of Henry Reynolds.

Fire of the Land (2002, 43 mins, VHS and DVD). A documentary set in Sydney during the 2000 Olympic Games, which tells the story of the Aboriginal Tent Embassy's peace camp in Victoria Park.

The First Australians (2008, SBS, DVD, available from Marcom Projects). A documentary on Aboriginal history from 1788 to the Mabo decision, in seven one-hour episodes. The early episodes focus on one region after another. It features interviews with scholars, readings from original sources and historic pictures.

First Citizen: Albert Namitjira (1989, VHS and DVD, 54 mins, available from Ronin Films). A documentary about the great artist and what his experiences show about Australia and Aboriginal policy in the 1950s.

How the West was Lost (1987, VHS and DVD, 72 mins, available from Ronin Films). A documentary about the Pilbara strike from 1946 onwards.

The Intervention (2008, DVD, 52 mins, available from Ronin Films). A documentary about the impact of the emergency intervention by the federal government in the Northern Territory region of Katherine, 2007–08.

Koories and Cops (1993, VHS and DVD, 30 mins, available from Ronin Films).

Documentary funded by the Victoria Police and Film Victoria as part of an improved cross-cultural awareness campaign which outlines the historical relationship between police and Aboriginal communities.

The Last Tasmanian (1978, 101 mins, DVD available from Ronin Films). Film by late archaeologist Dr Rhys Jones, this documentary covers prehistory and the twentieth century as well as the 'disappearance' of the Tasmanians between 1803 and 1876.

Link-Up Diary (1987, DVD, 90 mins, available from AIATSIS). On the effects of the removal of Aboriginal children by the New South Wales government. It follows a journey by three workers of Link-Up.

It's a Long Road Back (1981, film/DVD by Coral Edwards, 12 mins, available on DVD from AIATSIS). This film tells of the struggle of one woman taken from her family to regain her Aboriginality.

Lousy Little Sixpence (1982, colour and b&w, 55 mins, DVD available from Ronin Films). A documentary about life under the New South Wales Aborigines' Protection Board and the struggle against the board in the 1930s.

Mabo: Life of an Island Man (1997, film, 87 mins, DVD available from Film Australia). An award-winning documentary on Eddie Mabo and his case.

Mabo — The Native Title Revolution (2000, Film Australia Digital Learning production, combines CD-ROMs with a website and online database). This project brings together a documentary video with hundreds of specially created audiovisual sequences and a wealth of text and images from primary and secondary sources.

The Serpent and the Cross (1991, VHS and DVD, 55 mins, available from Ronin Films). This film features artists who are seeking to build bridges between the Dreaming and the Christian faith.

My Survival as an Aboriginal (1978, film, colour, 51 mins, 1978, DVD 2007), made by Essie Coffey (1940–98) and set around Brewarrina, NSW.

Vote Yes for Aborigines (2007, 52 mins, DVD available from Ronin Films). A documentary marking the 40th anniversary of the 1967 referendum; also about the fight for citizenship rights for Aborigines.

Walya Ngamardiki: The Land my Mother (1978, colour, 20 mins, Film Australia). About land, myths, sacred sites and uranium mining. Available online from www.filmaust.com.au.

Who Do You Think You Are? Catherine Freeman (2008, DVD, 52 mins, Film Australia). A part of the SBS-TV series on the family histories of celebrities. This one illustrates many typical aspects of Indigenous history in Queensland.

Women of the Sun (1981, series of four films, colour, each around 60 mins, on DVD from Ronin Films). These four stories about Aboriginal women span the period from the 1820s to the 1980s. A study guide is available. 1: Alinta the flame; 2: Maydina the shadow; 3: Nerida Anderson; 4: Lo-arna.

To Get That Country (1978, colour, 69 mins, 1978, available on DVD from AIATSIS). About the beginning of the Northern Lands Council.

Wrong Side of the Road (1981, film, DVD, colour, 79 mins, available from Ronin Films). Two Aboriginal rock groups, Us Mob and No Fixed Address, tour and perform.

Yorky Billy (1981, DVD, AIATSIS, 18 mins). The reminiscences of an elderly, now late, bushman in the Northern Territory.

Index

(Note: references to pictures are in *italics*)